www.wadsworth.com

wadsworth.com is the World Wide Web site for Wadsworth and is your direct source to dozens of online resources.

At *wadsworth.com* you can find out about supplements, demonstration software, and student resources. You can also send email to many of our authors and preview new publications and exciting new technologies.

wadsworth.com
Changing the way the world learns®

Wadsworth Developmental English

New for 2000

Writing

Robinson/Tucker, *Texts and Contexts: A Contemporary Approach to College Writing*, 4th Ed.
Tyner, *College Writing Basics: A Student-Writing Approach*, 5th Ed.
McDonald/Salomone, *The Writer's Response: A Reading-Based Approach to College Writing*, 2n[d]
McDonald/Salomone, *In Brief: A Handbook for Writers*

Reading

Maker/Lenier, *College Reading with the Active Critical Thinking Method, Book 1*, 5th Ed.
Maker/Lenier, *College Reading with the Active Critical Thinking Method, Book 2*, 6th Ed.
Sotiriou/Phillips, *Steps to Reading Proficiency*, 5th Ed.

Study Skills

Van Blerkom, *College Study Skills: Becoming a Strategic Learner*, 3rd Ed.

Other Developmental English Titles

Writing

Richard-Amato, *World Views: Multicultural Literature for Critical Writers, Readers, and Thinkers* (1998)
Salomone/McDonald, *Inside Writing: A Writer's Workbook, Form A*, 4th Ed. (1999)
Wingersky/Boerner/Holguin-Balogh, *Writing Paragraphs and Essays: Integrating Reading, Writing and Grammar Skills*, 3rd Ed. (1999)

Reading

Atkinson/Longman, *Reading Enhancement and Development*, 6th Ed. (1999)
Maker/Lenier, *Academic Reading with Active Critical Thinking* (1996)

Study Skills

Longman/Atkinson, *College Learning and Study Skills*, 5th Ed. (1999)
Longman/Atkinson, *Study Methods and Reading Techniques*, 2nd Ed. (1999)
Sotiriou, *Integrating College Study Skills: Reasoning in Reading, Listening, and Writing*, 5th Ed.
Smith/Knudsvig/Walter, *Critical Thinking: Building the Basics* (1998)

College Success

Gardner/Jewler, *Your College Experience: Strategies for Success*, 4th Ed. (2000)
Gardner/Jewler, *Your College Experience: Strategies for Success*, Concise 3rd Ed. (1998)
Holkeboer/Walker, *Right from the Start: Taking Charge of Your College Success*, 3rd Ed. (1999)
Petrie/Denson, *A Student Athlete's Guide to College Success: Peak Performance in Class and Life*
Santrock/Halonen, *Your Guide to College Success: Strategies for Achieving Your Goals* (1999)
Wahlstrom/Williams, *Learning Success: Three Paths to Being Your Best at College and Life*, 2nd (1999)

Patterns and Themes

A Basic English Reader

Fourth Edition

Judy R. Rogers
Georgetown College

Glenn C. Rogers
Georgetown College

Australia • Canada • Denmark • Japan • Mexico • New Zealand • Philippines • Puerto Rico
Singapore • South Africa • Spain • United Kingdom • United States

Executive Manager: Elana Dolberg
Senior Development Editor: Kim Johnson
Editorial Assistant: Godwin Chu
Marketing Assistant: Jessica McFadden
Project Editor: Christal Niederer
Print Buyer: Mary Noel
Permissions Editor: Joohee Lee
Production Service: Progressive Publishing Alternatives

Photo Researcher: Progressive Publishing Alternatives
Copy Editor: Progressive Publishing Alternatives
Compositor: Progressive Information Technologies
Cover Designer: Lisa Mirski Devenish/Devenish Design
Cover Image: PhotoDisc
Cover and Text Printer/Binder: Webcom Ltd.

COPYRIGHT © 2000 Wadsworth, a division of Thomson Learning. Thomson Learning is a trademark used herein under license.

All Rights Reserved. No part of this work may be reproduced, transcribed, or used in any form or by any means—graphic, electronic, or mechanical, including photocopying, recording, taping, Web distribution, or information storage and retrieval systems—without the prior written permission of the publisher.

Printed in Canada
1 2 3 4 5 6 7 03 02 01 00 99

For permission to use material from this text, contact us:
  Web: www.thomsonrights.com
  Fax: 1-800-730-2215
  Phone: 1-800-730-2214

Library of Congress Cataloging-in-Publication Data
Patterns and themes : a basic English reader/[compiled by] Judy R. Rogers, Glenn C. Rogers.—4th ed.
    p. cm.
    ISBN 0-534-26190-6
    1. College readers. 2. English language—Rhetoric Problems, exercises, etc. 3. English language—Grammar Problems, exercises, etc. 4. Report writing Problems, exercises, etc. 5. Basic English—Problems, exercises, etc. I. Rogers, Judy R.
    II. Rogers, Glenn C.
PE1417.P358   1999
808'.0427—dc21   99-16860

For more information, contact
Wadsworth/Thomson Learning
10 Davis Drive
Belmont, CA 94002-3098
USA
www.wadsworth.com

International Headquarters
Thomson Learning
290 Harbor Drive, 2nd Floor
Stamford, CT 06902-7477
USA

UK/Europe/Middle East
Thomson Learning
Berkshire House
168-173 High Holborn
London WC1V 7AA
United Kingdom

Asia
Thomson Learning
60 Albert Street #15-01
Albert Complex
Singapore 189969

Canada
Nelson/Thomson Learning
1120 Birchmount Road
Scarborough, Ontario M1K 5G4
Canada

Instructor's Edition: 0-534-26192-2

 This book is printed on acid-free recycled paper.

Thematic Table of Contents

Preface ~ xiii

Memories

Salvation ~ *Langston Hughes* **3**

Goals ~ *Curt Kruschwitz (student essay)* **9**

The Woman Warrior ~ *Maxine Hong Kingston* **13**

Down These Mean Streets ~ *Piri Thomas* **17**

Making a Mark on the World ~ *James A. Perkins* **23**

My First Hunting Trip ~ *John Bennett (student essay)* **31**

Families

My Family's Language ~ *Richard Rodriguez* **39**

Becoming Helpless ~ *Colette Dowling* **44**

The Great Sisters and Brothers War ~ *Andrew Shanley* **49**

Mrs. Razor ~ *James Still* **54**

Two Dads Are Better Than One? ~ *Angela Waugh (student essay)* **59**

Up the Hill ~ *Ryan Hardesty (student essay)* **62**

Laughter

After a Fall ~ *Garrison Keillor*   69
Pranks for the Memory ~ *Dave Barry*   75
The First Kiss ~ *Stephen Graves (student essay)*   79
Big Mike ~ *Jason Hanary (student essay)*   82

Differences

Halfway to Dick and Jane ~ *Jack Agueros*   89
Thoughts While Putting on Mascara Before Giving a Keynote Address ~ *Anne Barrett Swanson*   95
On Being Seventeen, Bright, and Unable to Read ~ *David Raymond*   99
For My Indian Daughter ~ *Lewis P. Johnson*   104

Sports

Head Down ~ *Stephen King*   113
Send Your Children to the Libraries ~ *Arthur Ashe*   117
Ex-Basketball Player ~ *John Updike*   122
Comes the Revolution ~ *Time*   125
Title IX: Bringing Equality to Athletics ~ *Jacquelyn Gist (student essay)*   130
Big, Dumb Jock ~ *Evan Carnes (student essay)*   134

Work

The Company Man ~ *Ellen Goodman*   141
Blue-Collar Journal ~ *John R. Coleman*   145
Out of Work in America ~ *Roger Rosenblatt*   150
Working Mothers ~ *Janet Krebs (student essay)*   154

Heroism

Where Have All the Heroes Gone? ~ *Pete Axthelm* **161**
A Personal Hero ~ *Bethany Hampton (student essay)* **168**
I Know Why the Caged Bird Sings ~ *Maya Angelou* **170**
Stride Toward Freedom ~ *Martin Luther King, Jr.* **175**

Women and Men

Yes, Women and Men Can Be "Just Friends" ~ *Marjorie Franco* **183**
Skiing with the Guys ~ *Catherine Ettlinger* **187**
Significant Other ~ *Rick Weiss* **194**
Keeping the Light On ~ *Leonard Pitts, Jr.* **200**
Women Wasted ~ *Jennifer Bitner (student essay)* **204**

Health

Wasted ~ *Marya Hornbacher* **211**
Talking AIDS to Death ~ *Randy Shilts* **217**
Driving Drunk ~ *Cecilia Kirtley (student essay)* **226**
Why Would Anyone Want to Smoke? ~ *Courtney Fugate (student essay)* **230**

Rhetorical Table of Contents

Description

Up the Hill ~ *Ryan Hardesty* **62**
After a Fall ~ *Garrison Keillor* **69**
Ex-Basketball Player ~ *John Updike* **122**
I Know Why the Caged Bird Sings ~ *Maya Angelou* **170**
Women Wasted ~ *Jennifer Bitner* **204**

Narration

Salvation ~ *Langston Hughes* **3**
The Woman Warrior ~ *Maxine Hong Kingston* **13**
Down These Mean Streets ~ *Piri Thomas* **17**
Making a Mark in the World ~ *James A. Perkins* **23**
My First Hunting Trip ~ *John Bennett* **31**
My Family's Language ~ *Richard Rodriguez* **39**
Up the Hill ~ *Ryan Hardesty* **62**
After a Fall ~ *Garrison Keillor* **69**
Pranks for the Memory ~ *Dave Barry* **75**
The First Kiss ~ *Stephen Graves* **79**
Halfway to Dick and Jane ~ *Jack Agueros* **89**

x Rhetorical Table of Contents

Thoughts While Putting on Mascara
Before Giving a Keynote Address ~ *Anne Barrett Swanson* **95**
Head Down ~ *Stephen King* **113**
Blue-Collar Journal ~ *John R. Coleman* **145**
I Know Why the Caged Bird Sings ~ *Maya Angelou* **170**
Skiing with the Guys ~ *Catherine Ettlinger* **187**
Wasted ~ *Marya Hornbacher* **211**

Illustration

The Company Man ~ *Ellen Goodman* **141**
On Being Seventeen, Bright, and Unable to Read ~ *David Raymond* **99**
Where Have All the Heroes Gone? ~ *Pete Axthelm* **161**
A Personal Hero ~ *Bethany Hampton* **168**
Yes, Women and Men Can Be "Just Friends" ~ *Marjorie Franco* **183**

Comparison/Contrast

Becoming Helpless ~ *Colette Dowling* **44**
Two Dads Are Better Than One? ~ *Angela Waugh* **59**
Thoughts While Putting on Mascara
Before Giving a Keynote Address ~ *Anne Barrett Swanson* **95**
Women Wasted ~ *Jennifer Bitner* **204**

Analysis

Halfway to Dick and Jane ~ *Jack Agueros* **89**
For My Indian Daughter ~ *Lewis P. Johnson* **104**
Out of Work in America ~ *Roger Rosenblatt* **150**
Skiing with the Guys ~ *Catherine Ettlinger* **187**
Significant Other ~ *Rick Weiss* **194**
Keeping the Light On ~ *Leonard Pitts, Jr.* **200**

Cause and Effect

Becoming Helpless ~ *Colette Dowling* 44

Out of Work in America ~ *Roger Rosenblatt* 150

Stride Toward Freedom ~ *Martin Luther King, Jr.* 175

Talking AIDS to Death ~ *Randy Shilts* 217

Persuasion

Thoughts While Putting on Mascara
Before Giving a Keynote Address ~ *Anne Barrett Swanson* 95

Send Your Children to the Libraries ~ *Arthur Ashe* 117

Title IX: Bringing Equality to Athletics ~ *Jacquelyn Gist* 130

Working Mothers ~ *Janet Krebs* 154

Yes, Women and Men Can Be "Just Friends" ~ *Marjorie Franco* 183

Driving Drunk ~ *Cecilia Kirtley* 226

Why Would Anyone Want to Smoke? ~ *Courtney Fugate* 230

For John and James

*who, rather like this text,
have grown and matured in unexpected and pleasing ways*

Preface

Since the third edition of *Patterns and Themes,* there have been important changes in basic writing—in students, in techniques, in materials, and probably in instructors. But though we may search for different and more effective ways of teaching, many of the challenges for basic writers remain the same. That is why the philosophy and overall design of *Patterns and Themes,* 4th edition, remain the same.

This text presents a collection of readings and writing assignments selected and designed to stimulate reader interest and to reinforce frequently used writing patterns. The content of the selections will appeal to a wide range of college readers, but the readability level is comfortable for basic writing students.

Rationale of *Patterns and Themes* Much has changed since the first edition appeared in 1985. Various movements and reforms in writing instruction have captured the attention of the profession and then faded away. Some of the voices we listened to in regional and national professional meetings are now silent; new, often younger, voices now share views, experiences, and the fruits of research. But as we have done in the Prefaces to the first three editions, so we now want to refer to that remarkably wise and humane pioneering work, Mina Shaughnessy's *Errors and Expectations.* It is still our intent to teach the integrated skills of writing, reading, and—we would add—thinking. We still hope that every student who uses this book will become the student Shaughnessy describes: "a more careful writer and a more critical reader."

Arrangement of the Text As in the past, the selections are first grouped by theme. For many students this arrangement provides a natural way to integrate material. Two themes from the third edition have been dropped; one new one has been added; other units have been expanded.

The themes are common to large groups of people from diverse backgrounds, and thus we have been able to provide varying points of view on the same topic. We hope that those who use this text will learn more about themselves, but even more important, that they will gain a better understanding of others who are different from them. The same essay may be a mirror for one reader and a window for another.

As before, the text offers variety of forms. There are sketches, short stories, selections from popular periodicals and excerpts from book-length works, student essays, and one brief poem. These readings cover a range of purposes from entertaining to informing to persuading and a range of emotions from mirth to anger to sorrow.

These selections fall rather naturally into a number of the traditional modes or patterns of writing, and as in earlier editions there is an alternative rhetorical table of contents. The modes have been in and out of favor over the years, but they do not go away. Many students, including many basic writers, find these organizational patterns helpful. These are understandable ways of organizing writing. Moreover, several are also well-established patterns or skills of critical thinking. As we have developed this text over a decade and a half, emphasizing the skills common to reading, writing, and thinking has become an increasingly important goal.

Learning Aids To increase students' enjoyment of the material and to speed the development of their reading and writing skills, we have included several learning aids.

"Looking Forward" gives brief biographical information about the authors (when relevant) and points students toward main ideas and important writing strategies.

"Help with Words" offers short definitions, often contextual, of many words that may be unfamiliar. We continue to believe that students are more successful when provided vocabulary help before, rather than after, the reading selections.

"A Second Look" sends students back to selections to consider points of meaning and to look again at writing techniques. Many of these questions can serve for group discussion as well as for individual consideration.

"Ideas for Writing" suggests writing assignment for paragraphs and, more often, short essays. In early units, the emphasis is on description and narration. Later assignments—like later reading selections—introduce definition, comparison/contrast, persuasion, and reports using outside sources, especially the Internet. Many of the assignments (especially early ones) are structured to help students move through the writing process.

"Making Connections" helps develop students' critical thinking skills while suggesting links among the essays in a unit. The questions and suggestions in "Making Connections" call upon students to compare, contrast, define, evaluate, identify values, recognize stereotypes, identify key issues, and perform other basic critical thinking tasks. The "connections" can also be used as a basis for small group or class discussion.

New to this Edition

- There are fifteen new selections, seven of which are student essays.
- "A Cyberlook" sends students to a variety of sites on the Internet or to specific subjects or essays available on *InfoTrac College Edition*.
- These Internet searches frequently provide the opportunity for collaborative work and even occasional collaborative writing assignments.
- Brief introductions to each theme suggest (or at least imply) why we feel the theme is important, and they often preview the essays.
- On the good advice of several instructors who have used the text, we have also included three student essays that respond to specific reading selections. This gives students the opportunity to see what "take" their peers have on an essay and how they deal with assigned topics or suggestions for writing.

Supplements

- **Instructor's Manual,** 0-534-26191-4. Includes complete instructor support including: readability level statistics; major rhetorical modes; overview of the readings; and tips for helping students interpret the reading and examine writing techniques. Also included are tips for using the InfoTrac and Internet activities.
- **InfoTrac® College Edition.** A fully searchable, online database with access to full-text articles from over 600 periodicals, provides a great resource for additional readings and/or research. A number of *Cyberlook* assignments in *Patterns and Themes* refer students to *Infotrac College Edition*. Now available for cost-effective bundling with this text, *InfoTrac College Edition* offers authoritative sources, updated daily and going back as far as four years. Both you and your students can receive unlimited online use for one academic term. (Please contact your Thomson Learning representative for policy, pricing, and availability; international and school distribution is restricted.)
- **Web Site.** Visit Wadsworth's Developmental English web site at http://devenglish.wadsworth.com. Here you will find a host of helpful services, including student and instructor resources, book-specific materials, and an online catalog.
- **Wadsworth Developmental English Internet at a Glance Trifold** (0-534-54744-3). This handy inexpensive guide shows your students where to find online reading and writing resources. Package this tri-

fold card with any Wadsworth Developmental English text for a very small cost. Contact your local Wadsworth representative for more information.

- **Custom Publishing.** You can combine your choice of chapters from specific Wadsworth titles with your own materials in a custom-bound book. To place your order, call the Thomson Learning Custom Order Center at 1-800-355-9983.
- **Videos.** Wadsworth has many videos available to qualifying adopters on topics such as improving your grades, notetaking practice, diversity and many more. Contact your local Wadsworth representative for more information.
- **AT&T World Net.** Get your students on the Internet with AT&T— one of the fastest growing Internet access service providers.

Acknowledgments

We wish to thank the reviewers who offered their suggestions for improving this edition:

Marie Franklin, Georgia Southern University;
William David Hall, Columbus State Community College;
Tim Miank, Lansing Community College;
Katherine Ploeger, California State University, Stanislaus;
Linda Ranucci, Kent State University;
Norman Stephens, Cerro Coso Community College; and
John Tyo, El Camino College.

And we wish to thank the staff at Wadsworth, especially Kim Johnson who, like all the editors we have worked work at Wadsworth, is characterized by patience and good cheer.

Memories

The selections in this unit generally tell of childhood experiences recalled by adult writers. While some experiences have more serious consequences than others, all show us how the adults we become are shaped and influenced by the children we were.

Salvation

Langston Hughes

Looking Forward

Langston Hughes—playwright, poet, fiction writer, expert in jazz and folklore—was one of the most influential figures in the history of African-American literature. In "Salvation," a section of his autobiography, Hughes recalls an experience from his youth that left him sad and disappointed. As you read, remember that a piece of writing should introduce and develop a main idea or central point. Hughes's main idea is introduced early. Watch for its development.

 Help with Words

fold *(paragraph 1):* a pen for sheep; here, a church or its congregation
escorted *(paragraph 1):* accompanied or led
rhythmical *(paragraph 3):* with regular accents or beats
dire *(paragraph 3):* dreadful
work-gnarled *(paragraph 4):* roughened or hardened from work
rounder *(paragraph 6):* a drunkard
serenely *(paragraph 7):* peacefully
knickerbockered *(paragraph 11):* wearing knickerbockers: short pants gathered at the knee
ecstatic *(paragraph 14):* greatly joyful, delighted

I was saved from sin when I was going on thirteen. But not really saved. It happened like this. There was a big revival at my Auntie Reed's church. Every night for weeks there had been much preaching, singing, praying, and shouting, and some very hardened sinners had been brought to Christ, and the membership of the church had grown by leaps and bounds. Then just before the revival ended, they held a special meeting for children, "to bring the young lambs to the fold." My aunt spoke of it for days ahead. That night I was escorted to the front row and placed on the mourners' bench with all the other young sinners, who had not yet been brought to Jesus.

My aunt told me that when you were saved you saw a light, and something happened to you inside! And Jesus came into your life! And God was with you from then on! She said you could see and hear and feel Jesus in your soul. I believed her. I had heard a great many old people say the same thing and it seemed to me they ought to know. So I sat there calmly in the hot crowded church, waiting for Jesus to come to me.

The preacher preached a wonderful rhythmical sermon, all moans and shouts and lonely cries and dire pictures of hell, and then he sang a song about the ninety and nine safe in the fold, but one little lamb was left in the cold. Then he said, "Won't you come? Won't you come to Jesus? Young lambs, won't you come?" And he held out his arms to all us young sinners there on the mourners' bench. And the little girls cried. And some of them jumped up and went to Jesus right away. But most of us just sat there.

A great many old people came and knelt around us and prayed, old women with jet-black faces and braided hair, old men with work-gnarled hands. And the church sang a song about the lower lights are burning, some poor sinners to be saved. And the whole building rocked with prayer and song.

Still I kept waiting to see Jesus.

Finally all the young people had gone to the altar and were saved, but one boy and me. He was a rounder's son named Westley. Westley and I were surrounded by sisters and deacons praying. It was very hot in the church, and getting late now. Finally Westley said to me in a whisper: "Goddamn! I'm tired o' sitting here. Let's get up and be saved." So he got up and was saved.

Then I was left all alone on the mourners' bench. My aunt came and knelt at my knees and cried, while prayers and songs swirled all around me in the little church. The whole congregation prayed for me alone, in a mighty wail of moans and voices. And I kept waiting serenely for Jesus, waiting, waiting—but he didn't come. I wanted to see him, but nothing happened to me. Nothing! I wanted something to happen to me, but nothing happened.

I heard the songs and the minister saying: "Why don't you come? My dear child, why don't you come to Jesus? Jesus is waiting for you. He wants you. Why don't you come? Sister Reed, what is this child's name?"

"Langston," my aunt sobbed.

"Langston, why don't you come? Why don't you come and be saved? Oh, Lamb of God! Why don't you come?"

Now it was really getting late. I began to be ashamed of myself, holding everything up so long. I began to wonder what God thought about Westley, who certainly hadn't seen Jesus either, but who was now sitting proudly on the platform, swinging his knickerbockered legs and grinning down at me, surrounded by deacons and old women on their knees praying. God had not struck Westley dead for taking his name in vain or for lying in the temple. So I decided that maybe to save further trouble, I'd better lie, too, and say that Jesus had come, and get up and be saved.

So I got up.

Suddenly the whole room broke into a sea of shouting, as they saw me rise. Waves of rejoicing swept the place. Women leaped into the air. My aunt threw her arms around me. The minister took me by the hand and led me to the platform.

When things quieted down, in a hushed silence, punctuated by a few ecstatic "Amens," all the new young lambs were blessed in the name of God. Then joyous singing filled the room.

That night, for the last time in my life but one—for I was a big boy twelve years old—I cried. I cried, in bed alone, and couldn't stop. I buried my head under the quilts, but my aunt heard me. She woke up and told my uncle I was crying because the Holy Ghost had come into my life, and because I had seen Jesus. But I was really crying because I couldn't bear to tell her that I had lied, that I had deceived everybody in the church, and I hadn't seen Jesus, and that now I didn't believe there was a Jesus any more, since he didn't come to help me.

6 *Memories*

 A Second Look

1. Pick out some descriptive words in paragraphs 3 and 4 that help you picture the scene in the church.

2. Hughes uses time order to organize his narrative. Transitional words at the beginnings of paragraphs emphasize this pattern. Locate these linking words at the beginning of paragraphs 5, 6, and 7. Are other paragraphs linked in this way?

3. Although writers usually avoid using one-sentence paragraphs except in reproducing speech, Hughes uses two (paragraphs 5 and 12). What does he achieve by doing this?

4. Why does young Hughes pretend to feel something that he has not really experienced?

5. Read the last paragraph again and state, in one sentence, why Hughes is crying.

 A Cyberlook

1. To learn more about Langston Hughes and his place in the history of American culture, search *InfoTrac College Edition* for Eric J. Sundquist, "Who Was Langston Hughes?"

2. Hughes was part of The Harlem Renaissance, a movement that helped shape American literature, music, and thought in the twentieth century. Search for "Harlem Renaissance" in *InfoTrac College Edition* and read the brief article from *The Reader's Companion to American History*.

3. In addition to print materials, a site called *Spotlight on Voices and Visions* gives video clips, audio presentations, and even a cybertour of Langston Hughes's hometown. Go to the *Learner Online* home page, click Search, enter "Langston Hughes," and then click on Voices and Visions. If your instructor wishes, you may work on this assignment in small groups and report on what you find. If you have difficulty finding the site, go to the *Wadsworth Developmental English* web page and click on Textbook Resource Centers.

 Ideas for Writing

Describe for a group of classmates something that happened to you when you were younger that left you frustrated or disappointed. Make sure your readers understand first what you expected to happen and then what actually happened.

After you choose the incident, write down everything you can remember about it. Do not worry about the order of your ideas or the mechanics of your writing. Just get your thoughts on paper. Then read through what you have written and select the details that seem most interesting and important. Mark these details so that you can refer to them later.

Next, decide how you will begin telling about your experience. Write the opening. Then continue describing the experience, using the details you have marked, until you reach the end. Your closing may explain why the incident was important. (Reread Hughes's last paragraph.)

Finally, reread your paper to see whether it says exactly what you want it to say. Make sure that the ideas are clear and that the details support the main idea.

Goals

Curt Kruschwitz

Looking Forward

Sometimes writing assignments based on essays in this text ask you to respond directly to points or ideas in the essays. More often, the writing topics are suggested by major ideas in the essays but not the specific content. Such is the Idea for Writing that follows Langston Hughes's "Salvation." Having read and discussed Hughes's essay about childhood confusion and disappointment, student writer Curt Kruschwitz wrote the following essay in response to the topic on pages 6–7, narrating and analyzing a very different but quite disappointing experience of his own. Look for differences between the experiences and the essays.

 Help with Words

ecstatic *(paragraph 3):* delighted, overjoyed, thrilled
devastated *(paragraph 5):* literally, destroyed; here (and often), bitterly
    disappointed or hurt

The game of soccer has always been important to me. Having played since first grade, I developed a passion for the sport at a young age. Particularly during middle school, soccer was my life. All the clothes that I wore had to do with soccer. I played every day after school. I helped coach my younger brother's soccer team. To make money on the weekends, I refereed youth soccer matches between the games that I played. Soccer consumed my life.

During my seventh grade year, I increased my level of commitment. I had been playing on recreational teams all my life; however, in seventh grade I decided I wanted to play on more competitive teams. I tried out and was selected to play for our local club team, the Richmond Strikers. That was definitely the highlight of my year. I loved playing for that team. The games were much more intense than in other leagues I had played in, and I enjoyed the challenge that was presented to me. Weekends were fun as we often traveled to out-of-town tournaments. I also enjoyed the status that came with playing for the Richmond Strikers—both my peers at school and other soccer players around the state knew that you had to be good to play for the Richmond Strikers.

The year flew by, and before I knew it, tryouts for the next season were announced. I knew immediately that I had a potential conflict with one of the dates. Tryouts were held on two afternoons, and on the first day my family had tickets to go to Washington D.C. to see the German national team play the Brazilian national team in U.S. Cup competition. Germany and Brazil are both soccer powerhouses, and I knew seeing them play live was a chance in a lifetime. I explained my situation to my coach and asked him if he thought it would be all right to miss my first tryout. He understood my situation and told me that he thought missing my first tryout would not hurt my chances for making the team for the second year. When I heard this, I was ecstatic for two reasons. First, I would get to watch a world-class soccer match. Second, I felt that I would definitely make the team again. After all, the coach wouldn't tell me it was OK to miss the tryout if there were a chance of my not making the team, would he?

That's what I thought. It turned out differently, though. I went to watch the Germany-Brazil match and thoroughly enjoyed it. However, when I came to my tryouts the second day, there was a different coach selecting our team than the one who had told me it would be OK to miss a day. This didn't bother me, however; I wasn't scared. I still felt that I was assured a spot on the team next season. That's not how it turned out.

About a month later, I received a letter thanking me for my interest in the Richmond Strikers but telling me that I wasn't selected for the team. I was devastated. I had not anticipated anything like this at all; it caught me totally off guard. All I did was sit and cry. I couldn't believe it. All sorts of thoughts ran through my head. Should I not have gone to the Germany-Brazil game? Did the new coach think I was not a good player? Had my old coach lied to me? Had he not put in a good word for me with the new coach? What was I to do now? I was ashamed to face my friends and tell them that I hadn't made the team. Making this team had meant so much to me. It seemed as if in an instant, my dreams had vanished.

Though it seemed horrible at the time, I think this situation 6 forced me to grow as a person. I learned that people aren't perfect. My old coach called and apologized; he really didn't know what to say. I also learned the value of hard work. I was determined to play for that team, so throughout the next season I worked out especially hard in order to prepare for the next tryout. Most important, I learned that there was more to life than soccer. Though I hadn't made the team I had hoped to, life went on. I still had friends, and I still had my family. I quickly learned that those were the important things in life and that they were enough to keep me going.

 A Second Look

1. The basic organization of Curt Kruschwitz's essay is chronological. How does he help his readers follow the time order of his narrative?

2. In paragraph 5, Kruschwitz asks himself a series of questions. Does he provide answers, either directly or indirectly? Is this an effective writing technique? Why or why not?

3. What were the positive effects of this disappointing experience?

4. Langston Hughes and Curt Kruschwitz are about the same age when they suffer disappointment, but there are not many other similarities. What is different about the causes, nature, and results of their experiences?

 Ideas for Writing

Write about an experience in your life—either positive or negative—that developed over a period of time. Like Curt Kruschwitz, you should provide background, narrate the experience, and explain the results or aftermath. Be sure to use clear time markers as transitional words and phrases so readers can follow the chronology of your narrative.

The Woman Warrior

Maxine Hong Kingston

Looking Forward

Maxine Hong Kingston, born in California to Chinese parents, has become one of the most important of the modern Chinese-American writers. She is the author of several books as well as a teacher of creative writing. In her autobiography, *The Woman Warrior,* Kingston recalls how, in her girlhood, she was caught between two cultures—the old one of China, which she had never seen, and the new one of America, which her family had not completely joined. In this selection, we see her growing rebellion against the harshly antifeminist attitudes of the emigrant Chinese.

 Help with Words

emigrant *(paragraph 5):* a person who has left one region or country to move to another

talking-story *(paragraph 11):* telling a story

grievances *(paragraph 12):* complaints

outward tendency *(paragraph 18):* refers to the usual custom among Chinese girls of leaving their families and becoming part of their husbands' families

My American life has been such a disappointment. 1

"I got straight A's, Mama." 2

"Let me tell you a true story about a girl who saved her 3 village."

I could not figure out what was my village. And it was 4 important that I do something big and fine, or else my parents

13

would sell me when we made our way back to China. In China there were solutions for what to do with little girls who ate up food and threw tantrums. You can't eat straight A's.

When one of my parents or the emigrant villagers said, "Feeding girls is feeding cowbirds," I would thrash on the floor and scream so hard I couldn't talk. I couldn't stop.

"What's the matter with her?"

"I don't know. Bad, I guess. You know how girls are. 'There's no profit in raising girls. Better to raise geese than girls'."

"I would hit her if she were mine. But then there's no use wasting all that discipline on a girl. 'When you raise girls, you're raising children for strangers'."

"Stop that crying!" my mother would yell. "I'm going to hit you if you don't stop. Bad girl! Stop!" I'm going to remember never to hit or to scold my children for crying, I thought, because then they will only cry more.

"I'm not a bad girl," I would scream. "I'm not a bad girl. I'm not a bad girl." I might as well have said, "I'm not a girl."

"When you were little, all you had to say was 'I'm not a bad girl,' and you could make yourself cry," my mother says, talking-story about my childhood.

I minded that the emigrant villagers shook their heads at my sister and me. "One girl—and another girl," they said, and made our parents ashamed to take us out together. The good part about my brothers being born was that people stopped saying, "All girls," but I learned new grievances. "Did you roll an egg on my face like that when I was born?" "Did you have a full-month party for me?" "Did you turn on all the lights?" "Did you send my picture to Grandmother?" "Why not? Because I'm a girl? Is that why not?" "Why didn't you teach me English?" "You like having me beaten up at school, don't you?"

"She is very mean, isn't she?" the emigrant villagers would say.

"Come, children. Hurry. Hurry. Who wants to go out with Great-Uncle?" On Saturday mornings my great-uncle, the ex-river pirate, did the shopping. "Get your coats, whoever's coming."

"I'm coming. I'm coming. Wait for me."

When he heard girls' voices, he turned on us and roared, "No girls!" and left my sisters and me hanging our coats back up, not looking at one another. The boys came back with candy and new toys. When they walked through Chinatown, the people must have said, "a boy—and another boy—and another boy!" At my great-uncle's funeral I secretly tested out feeling glad that he was dead—the six-foot bearish masculinity of him.

I went away to college—Berkeley in the sixties—and I studied, and I marched to change the world, but I did not turn into a boy. I would have liked to bring myself back as a boy for my parents to welcome with chickens and pigs. That was for my brother, who returned alive from Vietnam.

If I went to Vietnam, I would not come back; females desert families. It was said, "There is an outward tendency in females," which meant that I was getting straight A's for the good of my future husband's family, not my own. I did not plan ever to have a husband. I would show my mother and father and the nosey emigrant villagers that girls have no outward tendency. I stopped getting straight A's.

 A Second Look

1. Why is Kingston's family not impressed that young Maxine got straight A's?
2. Explain what Kingston means in paragraph 10.
3. What kinds of distinctions does the family make between sons and daughters?
4. In what ways does Kingston rebel against the culture that rejected her? Why does she choose the strategy she does?

 A Cyberlook

1. Elsewhere in *The Woman Warrior* Kingston explains that part of the conflict with her family grew out of language. The younger generation spoke only English; the older generation usually spoke Chinese, often using their native language for private conversations that they did not want the children to understand. Many immigrant families face this language problem. Search *InfoTrac College Edition* for "Chinese Americans" and read Victoria Chen, "Chinese American women, language, and moving subjectivity."

2. You will find many and various Internet sites with information on Maxine Hong Kingston. Working in small groups, spend a few minutes exploring some of the sites and compare results. Report on any especially interesting sites you discover. (You may find one or more Kingston web pages created by students enrolled in English classes.)

 Ideas for Writing

Have you ever been in serious disagreement with the attitudes and beliefs of your family? Write about this situation, telling your readers (a group of people your own age) what these beliefs were and describing how you rebelled against them. Your essay should give clear answers to these questions:

1. What were the beliefs you and your family disagreed over?

2. How did you and the family express your feelings? Give examples.

3. Were you able to settle these differences? If so, how? If not, what have been the results of your continued disagreement?

Down These Mean Streets

Piri Thomas

Looking Forward

Piri Thomas was born to Puerto Rican parents in Spanish Harlem. In his twenties, Thomas, a drug user, was imprisoned for attempted armed robbery. Cured of his addiction and released from prison, he became a drug rehabilitation worker in Spanish Harlem and Puerto Rico. In an early chapter of his autobiography, *Down These Mean Streets*, Thomas writes about his hatred of school and teachers. In this selection, he tells about one of his many conflicts in the classroom. Notice how this street-smart kid can turn a bad situation partly to his own advantage.

 Help with Words

muted *(paragraph 15)*: quiet
Qué pasa? *(paragraph 17)*: What's the matter? What's going on? (Spanish)
chastised *(paragraph 20)*: punished
intention *(paragraph 25)*: wish, purpose
discretion *(paragraph 39)*: caution
valor *(paragraph 39)*: bravery
padre *(paragraph 41)*: father (Spanish)
muchacho *(paragraph 43)*: boy, son (Spanish)

One class I didn't dig at all was the so-called "Open Air Class" for skinny, "underweight" kids. We had to sleep a couple of half hours every day, and we got extra milk and jelly and peanut butter on brown bread. The teacher, Miss Shepard, was like a dried-up grape. One day I raised my hand to go to the toilet, but she paid me no mind. After a while, the pain was getting bad, so I called out, "Miss Shepard, may I leave the room?"

She looked up and just shook her head, no.

"But I gotta go, Miss Shepard."

"You just went a little while ago," she said.

"I know, Miss Shepard, but I gotta go again."

"I think it's sheer nonsense," said the old bitch. "You just want an excuse to play around in the hallways." ...

I had to go so badly that I felt the tears forming in the corners of my eyes to match the drops that were already making a wet scene down my leg. "I'm goin' anyway," I said, and started toward the door.

Miss Shepard got up and screamed at me to get back to my seat. I ignored her.

"Get back to your seat, young man," she screamed. "Do you hear me? Get right back—" ...

I reached the door and felt her hands grab out at me and her fingers hook on to the back of my shirt collar. My clean, washed-a-million-times shirt came apart in her hand.

I couldn't see her face clearly when I turned around. All I could think about was my torn shirt and how this left me with only two others. All I could see was her being the cause of the dampness of my pants and hot pee running down my leg. All I could hear was the kids making laughing sounds and the anger of my being ashamed. I didn't think of her as a woman, but as something that had to be hit. I hit it. ...

"You struck me! You *struck* me! Oh, help, help!" she cried.

I cut out. Man, I ran like hell into the hallway, and she came right after me, yelling, "Help, help!" I was scared now and all I could think about was getting back to my Moms, my home, my block, where no one could hurt me. I ran toward the stairway and found it blocked off by a man, the principal. I cut back toward the back stairs.

"Stop him! Stop him!" dear Miss Shepard yelled, pointing her finger at me. "He struck me, he struck me."

I looked over my shoulder and saw the principal talk to her for a hot second and then take off after me, yelling: "Stop! Stop!" I hit the stairs and went swooming down like it was all one big step. The principal was fast and I could hear him swearing right behind me. I slammed through the main-floor door that led to the lunchroom and jumped over benches and tables, trying like hell to make the principal trip and break a leg. Then I heard a muted cry of pain as a bench caught him in the shin. I looked over my shoulder and I dug his face. The look said that he was gonna hit me; that he wasn't gonna listen to my side of the story; that I had no side. I figured I better not get caught.

I busted my legs running toward the door that led to the outside and freedom, and with both hands out in front of me I hit the brass bar that opens the door. Behind me I heard a thump as the principal smacked into it. I ran down the block, sneaking a look behind me. The principal was right behind me, his face redder and meaner. People were looking at the uneven contest.

I tore into my hallway, screaming as loud as I could for help. The apartment doors opened up, one right after another. Heads of all colors popped out. "*Qué pasa?*" asked a Puerto Rican woman. "Wha's happenin'?" said a colored lady.

"They wanna beat me up in school and that's one of them," I puffed, pointing at the principal, who was just coming into view.

"Hooo, ain't nobody gonna hurt you, sonny," said the colored lady, whose name was Miss Washington. She gently pushed me behind her with one hand and with the other held it out toward the principal roaring down at us.

The principal, blocked by Miss Washington's 280 pounds and a look of "Don't you touch that boy," stopped short and puffed out, "That—that—kid—he—punched a teacher and—he's got to be chastised for it. After all, school disci—"

"Now hol' on, white man," Miss Washington interrupted. "There ain't nobody gonna chaz—whatever it is—this boy. I knows him an' he's a good boy—at least good for what comes outta this heah trashy neighborhood—an' you ain't gonna do nuttin' to him, unless you-all wan's to walk over me."

Miss Washington was talking real bad-like. I peeked out from behind that great behind.

"Madam, I assure you," the principal said, "I didn't mean harming him in a bodily manner. And if you knew the whole issue, you would agree with me that he deserves being chastised. As principal of his school, I have his best interest at heart. Ha, ha, ha," he added, "you know the old saying, madam, 'A stitch in time saves nine.' Ha, ha, ha—*ahurmph.*"

I could see him putting that stitch in my head.

"I assure you, madam," he continued, smilingly pretty, "we have no intention of doing him bodily harm."

Once again I peeked out from behind Miss Washington's behind. "Yeah, that's what you say," I said. "How about alla time you take kids down to your office for some crap and ya start poking 'em with that big finger of yours until they can't take it anymore?"

There were a lot of people in the hall by this time. They were all listening, and I knew it. "Yeah, ask any of the kids," I added. "They'll tell ya." I looked sorry-like at the crowd of people, who were now murmuring mean-like and looking at the principal like he didn't have long on this earth.

Smelling a Harlem lynch party in the making, I said, "An'— you—ain't—gonna—do—it—to—me. I'll get me a forty-five an'—"

"Hush you mouth, boy," Miss Washington said; "don't be talkin' like that. We grownups will get this all straightened out. An' nobody's gonna poke no finger in your chest"—she looked dead at the principal—"is they?"

The principal smiled the weakest smile in this smiling world. "I—I—I—er, assure you, madam, this young man is gifted with the most wonderful talent for prevarication I've ever seen."

"What's that mean?" Miss Washington asked suspiciously.

"Er, it means a good imagination, madam. A-ha-ha—yes, *ahurmph.*"

"That's a lie, Miss Washington," I said. "He's always telling the kids that. We asked Mrs. Wagner, the history teacher, and she said it means to lie. Like he means I'm a liar."

The look in the principal's eye said, "Oh, you smarty pants bastard," but he just smiled and said nothing.

Miss Washington said, "Iffen thar's any pokin' ta be done, we all heah is gonna do it," and she looked hard at the principal. The crowd looked hard at the principal. Hard sounds were taking forms, like, "So this is the way they treat our kids in school?" and

"What you-all expect? These heah white people doan give a damn," and "If they evah treats mah boy like that, I'd . . . ."

The principal, smiling softly, began backing up.

I heard Momma's voice: "Piri, Piri, *qué pasa?*"

"Everything all right, Mis' Thomas," Miss Washington assured her. "This heah man was tryin' to hit your son, but ain't, 'cause I'll break his damn head wide open." Miss Washington shifted her weight forward. "Damn, Ah got a good mind to do it right now," she added.

The principal, remembering the bit about discretion being the better part of valor, split.

Everyone tried to calm Moms down. I felt like everybody there was my family. I let Momma lead me upstairs to our apartment. Everyone patted me on the head as we went by.

"You're going to school with your *padre* in the morning," Momma said.

"Uh-uh, Moms," I said. "That principal will stomp my chest in with that finger of his."

"No he won't, *muchacho*. Your father will go with you an' everything will be fixed up."

I just nodded my head and thought how great it would be if Miss Washington could go with me.

A Second Look

1. Thomas uses much direct quotation in his writing. How does he make the voices of Miss Shepard, the principal, and Miss Washington sound different?

2. How is the voice or style of the narrator (the adult Thomas) different from the voice of the student (young Piri)?

3. At the end of paragraph 11, Thomas says, "I hit it." Why does he use the pronoun *it* instead of *her*?

4. What does Thomas mean when he says he smells "a Harlem lynch party in the making" (paragraph 28)? Is he exaggerating?

5. Miss Washington and the principal take sides and act quickly in this situation because they act on the basis of group values that they have accepted. What are these values in each case?

A Cyberlook

Though *Down These Mean Streets* is Thomas's best-known work, he has written a great deal over a long period of time. To learn more about his life and work (including some photographs of Thomas from childhood to the present), access his home page. If you have difficulty finding the site, go to the *Wadsworth Developmental English* web page and click on Textbook Resource Centers.

Ideas for Writing

1. Tell about a situation in school or elsewhere in which you found yourself in trouble with those in authority. Begin by setting up the circumstances and introducing the people you will write about. (Notice that Thomas describes Miss Shepard briefly. He doesn't describe the principal at first; we learn about the principal through what he says and does.) Then show how the situation developed, what actions took place, and how it ended.

2. Describe a teacher you liked or disliked very much. You will want to tell what the teacher looked like, how he or she behaved in class, and why you liked or disliked this person. You may use brief stories to help your readers understand what kind of person the teacher was.

3. Look at paragraphs 15 and 16 of Thomas's narrative. His description is alive and exciting because he uses many active, lively verbs. Try writing a paragraph in which you describe some brief but vigorous physical action—for example, running through a crowded place, lifting a heavy weight, passing a football, serving in tennis, chasing or being chased by an animal. Use as many lively and specific verbs as you can.

Making a Mark on the World

James A. Perkins

Looking Forward

In this short story, James Perkins—a college teacher and author of essays, stories, poems, and radio and TV scripts—recalls a childhood opportunity to "make his mark." As often happens, this youthful experience has implications that the adult writer understands only years later. In fact, what may be the most important point of the story is implied, not directly stated: It is human nature to want to make a mark, to leave something which will assure that others know we were here; but there may be a price to pay for making a mark, and the decision whether to make it responsibly is up to us.

Help with Words

Greenline car barn *(paragraph 21):* a storage and repair facility for street cars (the Greenline)
viscous *(paragraph 24):* thick, sticky
Inner Sanctum *(paragraph 42):* an old radio program that featured a famous, spooky sound: a loudly creaking door that closed with a metallic slam

When I stepped off the trolley with my mother, I saw Mr. Johnson breaking up his sidewalk with a sledge hammer. I started walking toward him.

"James, you get right in the house and remove your good clothes. What are you thinking of?"

I knew exactly what I was thinking of—fresh concrete—but I couldn't tell my mother that.

"Yes'm," I said.

"What do you mean, James? 'Yes' does not tell me what you are thinking."

"I mean, 'Yes'm, I'll go in and change my clothes.' Then can I go play with Bobby?"

"May I go play."

"Yes'm. May I go play with Bobby?"

"You may, but stay within earshot. It won't be long till lunch."

I knew my secret interest in fresh concrete was safe because when my mother started a grammar lesson, her mind was clouded to everything else. For an hour Bobby and I watched Mr. Johnson breaking concrete with a sledge hammer, and we followed him as he rolled it to the woods in a wheelbarrow to fill in a gully and halt erosion.

"You boys know what I'm doing here?"

"You're hauling that concrete into the woods."

"I'm making my mark in the world. I'm trying to leave this earth a better place than I found it. It was only given to us to watch."

"What, sir?" I asked.

"The earth, boy. It was given to us to watch. And look at it. We're going to bury it in trash."

Of all the things Mr. Johnson said, the thing that stuck with us was the idea of making a mark in the world. In front of Summe and Ratterman's Dairy, the city had put in a new sidewalk after a water main broke and caved in the street. The McCoy Street Gang, every last one of them, wrote their names in the wet concrete with a nail. We read them every time we went to the dairy for ice cream.

"No better than a pack of dogs pissing on bushes," my father said the first time he saw the names. I had seen dogs sniffing up and down the alley behind our house to see if any other dogs were moving into their area, and pissing to remind intruders that our alley already had enough dogs. The McCoy Street Gang carved an eye in phone poles to show where their land began, just behind Nielander's Saloon. Sometimes we walked back there and looked at the eye, but we never went past it. Hoboes did. Hoboes went everywhere.

Hoboes were men who lived down by the Licking River in camps, men who couldn't hold jobs, even during the war—men who didn't want jobs. They left messages for each other in chalk on the sidewalks the way the pioneers had blazed trails through the Kentucky woods with axe marks. We weren't allowed to mark the trees in Mr. Johnson's woods.

"You might damage the tree, Son," my father said. "When Daniel Boone and Simon Kenton were wandering through here, we had a lot more trees than people. Not any more."

The hoboes' messages were in a code we couldn't crack, but one of the signs had to do with our kitchen and my mother's pies. Almost every time my mother baked, a chalk mark appeared on our corner, and a few men drifted up to our back door for a wedge of apple or rhubarb pie and a cup of coffee.

Then there was Kilroy, whoever he was. His name was painted on the side of the cinder block garages behind Nancy's house: "KILROY WAS HERE." He was also in the alley behind Schulte and Wisher's and in the new concrete up in front of the Greenline car barn on Madison at Twentieth. Kilroy had made his mark on the world, and we would, too.

After lunch Bobby and I sat on the curb in front of my house with tenpenny nails curled in our palms, waiting.

Mr. Johnson put down a bed of gravel in the wooden forms he'd built, and tamped and leveled it. About three o'clock the Tate Builders Supply company's huge orange and black concrete mixer groaned up the narrow street.

Mr. Johnson and the driver swung the chute into place over the waiting gravel, and viscous gray concrete slid down the chute into the form. Mr. Johnson jiggled and prodded the mass to make sure it filled all the nooks and crannies, then he and the driver ran a two-by-four across the top of the form to level the concrete.

After the truck rolled away, Mr. Johnson splashed water on the surface of the walk and began working a swirling pattern into it with a toothed trowel. By this time, Bobby and I were standing with our toes next to the form, our tenpenny nails burning holes in our palms.

"See, boys, I put a little texture in the wet concrete so it will be a little rough when it dries. That will make it better to walk on, especially when it gets wet. If you leave it smooth, it's slick as glass when it rains."

After he finished with his trowel, he sprayed the walk with a fine mist from his garden hose. Bobby and I wanted to put some texture in that sidewalk, but Mr. Johnson picked up his evening paper and sat down on a lawn chair right there by the fresh concrete. We went back to my porch to consider our situation.

We were stuck. If we were going to be immortal, have our names in concrete, be as famous as the McCoy Street Gang or Kilroy, we were going to have to employ a strategy.

When Billy came by a little later, he put the problem in a nutshell.

"Geez, Four-eyes, we'll have to go to bed before he moves off that chair, and tomorrow that walk will be so hard we'd have to blast our names into it."

"Tonight," I said.

"Tonight, what?"

"Tonight, we'll sneak out and do it."

"When, Four-eyes?"

"Midnight."

I said my goodnights, and my mother tucked me into bed. After she left, I took my clothes out of the hamper, dressed, strapped on my six guns, and pulled on my Red Ryder gloves. I stuck the nail into my gun belt and lay back down on my bed. I was barely able to stay awake, but when the bell in the chapel tower at the hospital at the end of the street struck twelve, I opened my window and went across the porch roof and down the drain pipe to wait for Billy under the streetlight by the car tracks. I knew better than to expect Bobby. He had told me he was going to stay home.

Billy didn't come, either.

When the hospital clock struck one, I was still standing under the streetlight watching the stars. Billy wasn't coming.

Whatever I was going to do to Mr. Johnson's new concrete walk, I was going to do it on my own. Billy was probably sound asleep, and I was under the street lamp watching the bats dart around the house roofs in the moonlight.

I had stayed up to see the New Year in once, but I had never been up this late in my life. On New Year's Eve, I sat in my father's big leather chair in the front room and drank punch while my aunt and uncle danced, and my mother and father smiled and drank coffee and said it had been a good year, all things considered.

That was midnight and indoors. This was one o'clock outdoors, and I couldn't seem to step out of the glare of the street light into the strange light of the moon.

There were sounds. Night sounds. Some of them, like the ear-close buzz of a mosquito or the far-off mournful hoot of an owl, I knew. But there were other sounds. Rustlings and cracks and chunks and hisses that I had never heard before. The wind caught the gate in Nancy's yard and swung it slowly shut like the door on Inner Sanctum.

I slapped leather and went into a crouch with the six gun in my left hand leveled toward the sound. I was reaching with my slower right hand toward the butt of the other gun when I realized I didn't even have any caps. I had nothing to protect me from the fear and evil and death which rode the night air as clearly as bats.

I stepped, utterly defenseless, from the ring of street light and walked to Mr. Johnson's fresh concrete with only a nail gripped in the cotton of my Red Ryder glove. I knelt at the corner of the walk and raised the nail, ready to drive my name deep into the concrete, deep into time.

Then I froze. I could not move. Two thoughts crossed my mind, and I was paralyzed. If I wrote my name on Mr. Johnson's walk, I would be famous and well known—especially to Mr. Johnson, who would tell my father, to whom I already felt myself to be sufficiently notorious.

The second thought was less precise, but it affected me much more. It was a memory, a memory of the day of my grandfather's funeral.

They had lowered my grandfather into a grave next to his first wife. Their names were already carved in the headstone. Her dates were complete. His birth date waited alone for the numbers which could now be worked into the stone.

My father and I walked backward in time through the graveyard as he pointed out relatives whose names were increasingly difficult to read on the weather-worn stones.

"This is your great-grandfather Huddleston. He wore himself out, wearing out land too poor to harvest rocks from. He once cropped it to death with tobacco. It's nothing but gullies and washes now, and he's here."

I knew then I'd have my name in stone soon enough, and I knew now that there were better things to do than to try to fix yourself in time by what you did. I leaned forward and pressed the thumb of my Red Ryder glove into the hardening concrete. A small mark, a thumb print masked by the cotton of the gloves so that even Dick Tracy and the crimestoppers couldn't lift the print from the dried concrete. My mission was complete.

I moved more lightly through the night, back to my window. I pulled at it, but it had slid shut. I couldn't raise the sash. I pried it with the barrel of my six gun. It would not budge. I was out for the rest of the night.

I slid back down the drain pipe and sat on the porch swing, thinking, all night. I sat very still because the swing made an awful screech when it moved, and although the night was lonely, I didn't really want to see my parents just then.

I thought about a lot of things, about the differences between the street light and the moonlight and how dark it was between the stars. I thought about how the noises in the darkness scared me. I thought about a lot of things. Mr. Johnson was right. A man should leave the earth a better place. Bobby and I would spend the summer picking up trash along the street and the car track. It would be neat. The car tracks would be cleaner, and we would find pop bottles that were worth two cents apiece at Wiemann's Store.

By the time I had expanded the plan to include Billy and the clean-up of Garrad Street, the birds were chirping in the morning light, and my eyes were heavy. Then I heard the milkman turning the corner of the street. I scampered down the steps and around the corner of the house. Our milkman didn't miss much. He saw me duck around the corner, and as he picked up the empties next to the tin cooler box, he whispered, "I see you around there, boy. What are you doing tom-catting around at this time of the morning?"

I didn't say anything, and he put our milk into the box.

"If you're going to get up this early, you might as well come over to the dairy and help me work. At my age, I need a good tom cat to keep up my reputation." He laughed and went back to his truck.

After he left, I heard my mother open the door and take the milk in for breakfast. I wanted to give her time to get back to the kitchen, then slipped up the steps and across the porch and through the door as quietly as I could. I crossed the living room and dining room and was halfway up the stairs when I heard her returning from the kitchen. I spun around on the stairs and bounded down the way I did every morning.

"Morning, Mom. What's for breakfast?" 58

"Oatmeal," she said, placing a tray of steaming bowls on the 59 table. "You're up early and already dressed." Then she seemed to notice something wrong. "James, those are the same clothes you had on yesterday afternoon. You go right back upstairs and change. Hurry. This oatmeal will get cold."

"Yes'm." 60

A Second Look

1. This story contains a great deal of dialogue. How does Perkins make the conversations sound natural and appropriate for the young narrator?

2. Occasionally the narrator seems to wander away from his story. Find one of two of these short digressions and determine whether they are actually related to the writer's main point.

3. The phrase "making a mark on the world" is used to mean more than one thing in this story. Explain.

4. How does young Jim ("Four-eyes" to his friends) finally make his mark? Why is this plan more satisfactory than the original one?

5. Perkins could have ended his story with paragraph 53 or within paragraph 54. Why do you think he concludes his narrative as he does?

Ideas for Writing

1. Writing gains interest and power from specific details and a lively vocabulary, especially from interesting verbs. Look at paragraphs 17, 20, 24, 36, 42, 53, and 54 in Perkins's story. Then write a descriptive paragraph on any topic you choose, paying special attention to your choice of words and details.

2. Write a narrative based on a childhood experience that seemed daring and dangerous at the time, even though it may appear tame to you as an adult writer.

My First Hunting Trip

John Bennett

Looking Forward

This essay was written by a freshman composition student. As in Langston Hughes's "Salvation," the main idea here concerns the difference between what Bennett expected and what really happened. To make his point, he emphasizes how he feels at different times during the hunting trip.

Help with Words

foraging *(paragraph 6):* searching for food
replica *(paragraph 6):* a copy
mauling *(paragraph 11):* injuring by rough treatment

It seems as if the cold is what I remember most. 1

The three of us (Tom, Dad, and I) rode in Tom's old pickup, 2 sitting on our hands to keep them warm. I had been on hunting trips before, but this one was different. For the first time, I was allowed to carry a gun—an overused Winchester 20-gauge that was nearly as big as I was.

There was snow on the ground—three, maybe four inches. 3 The drive to our old farm was painfully long, but we arrived just before dawn. We quickly unpacked, loaded our guns, and headed along an old road toward a dense group of briars, fallen trees, and young saplings. The two beagles we had brought along as "flushers" scurried from tree to bush, eagerly sniffing some day-old scent.

When we reached the top of the hill, two rabbits broke behind us. My dad and Tom shot once apiece, missing each time. I mumbled something about being too cold to move and walked on.

My task, I soon learned, was to sit and wait at the edge of the dense forest while Tom and Dad took the two dogs in. Supposedly, they would flush the rabbits out so I could get a shot. It sounded a bit suspicious to me, but I was tired from walking anyway.

I watched them disappear into the brush and sat down on a damp, rotten log. I then concentrated on observing the tree line I was stationed upon; no movement, not even the slightest change went unnoticed. After a while, large clumps of grass began to imitate foraging rabbits. Only a sudden gust of wind saved one extremely life-like replica, some forty-five yards away.

I laid my gun on one side of the log and put both my hands inside my wool jacket in a fruitless attempt to keep them warm. It was no use; my fingers became numb and lifeless. There was no shelter from the wind, and every five minutes or so I would shake my arms like an injured bird, trying to create some body heat.

Up ahead, about seventy-five yards, the smaller of the two dogs came out of the foliage, ran toward me for twenty feet, and then was lost again in the brush. He was obviously on to something.

I suddenly became unaware of the cold as I reached for my gun. The same fingers that just before were blue and numb clicked the safety off. Trying to get a better look, I stood up above the weeds. I felt my heart quicken its pace, and I felt myself begin to tremble. Not from cold, however—I was no longer cold—but I trembled with an anticipation of what I somehow knew would come. I loosened the top button of my hunting vest and waited.

The rabbit appeared about fifty yards away, oblivious to my presence. I knew it was too far away for a certain kill shot, so I slowly knelt down and tried to hide. The rabbit, intent on escaping from the dog on its trail, came directly toward me until it was in range. I rose, ready for my prey to bolt away in fear. Instead, the rabbit continued toward me, and then stopped five yards away from the gun barrel pointed at its head. It sat there, partially obscured by the snow, mocking the fact that I held its life in my right index finger.

I was confused, uncertain. This wasn't how it was supposed to be, not how I had seen it before. There was no sport (a favorite hunter's word) in mauling a rabbit sitting fifteen feet away. The rabbit wouldn't move, even when I stomped my foot in the snow.

I could not let my chance pass. Bracing myself for the recoil of my weapon, I squeezed the trigger and watched my prey fall into the blood-stained snow.

My trembling had stopped, and I realized that my bottom layer of clothes was soaked with perspiration. I sat down beside the rabbit, watching its back legs writhe violently.

"Reflexes," I told myself.

Tom and Dad approached me from behind. Seeing the rabbit, now still and cold in the snow, they congratulated me on my first kill. I watched Tom field dress the rabbit as he told me of his first rabbit.

I wasn't listening much. It had become cold again, and I turned my back to the wind.

A Second Look

1. Bennett emphasizes the cold beginning with the first sentence. What details indicate how cold he feels? Why does he feel cold again after shooting the rabbit?

2. What other kinds of details does the author use in the first three paragraphs?

3. What does paragraph 6 indicate about the author's state of mind? (Note that he shows us rather than tells us.)

Ideas for Writing

1. Write a paragraph describing a time when you were unusually cold, hot, or wet, for instance. Concentrate on using sense words. To get started, list as many words as you can think of that describe how you felt. Choose several of the most vivid ones to include in your paragraph.

2. Write about an important experience in your life that taught you something about yourself. Be sure that the main idea is clear, even if it is not stated in your essay.

Making Connections

The essays of Langston Hughes, Maxine Hong Kingston, James Perkins, and John Bennett all recall disillusioning experiences that left the young people with a feeling different from the one their cultures had led them to expect. Is the disillusionment necessary to their growing up? Does each young person learn some important reality?

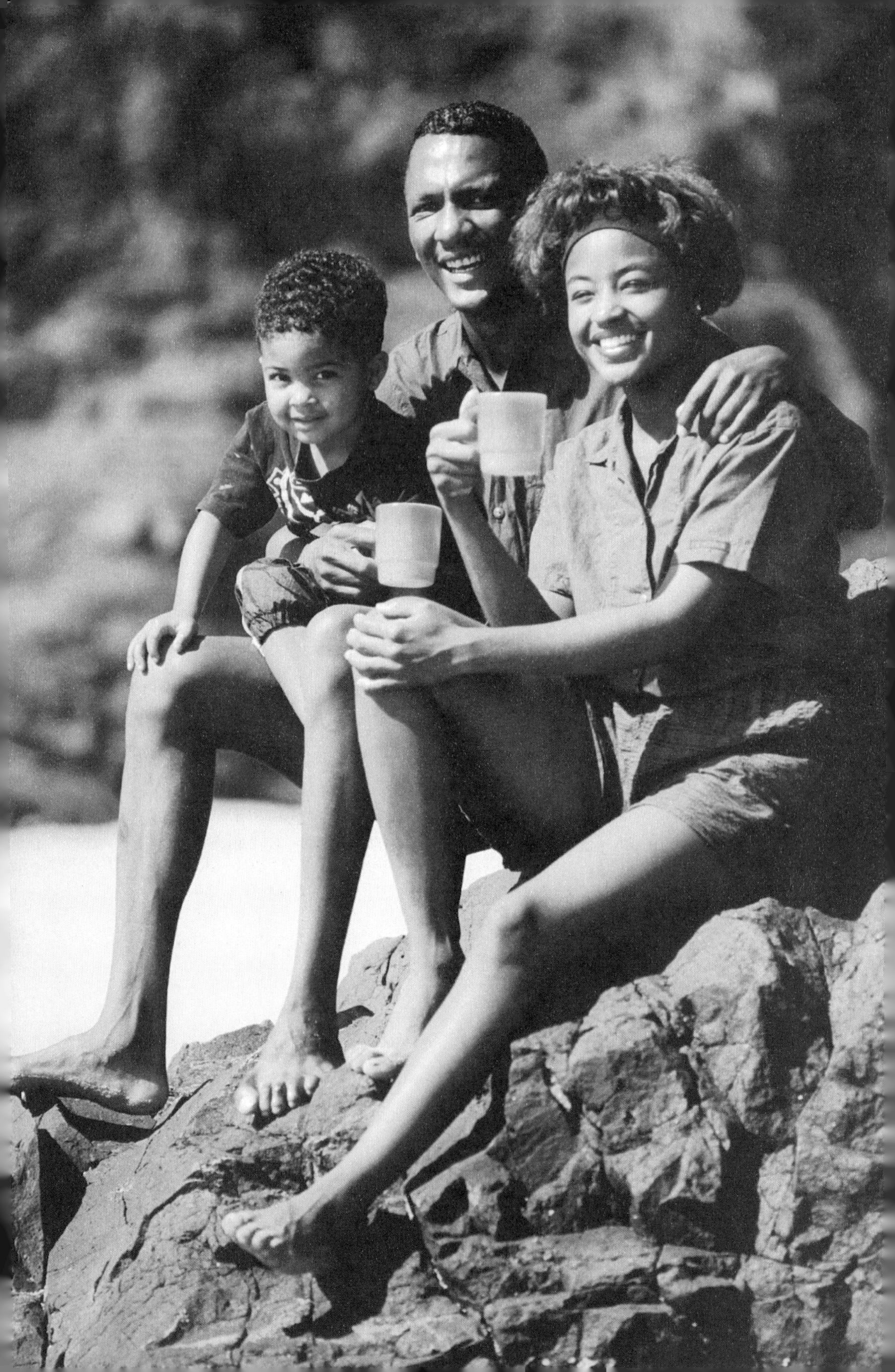

Families

Though we come from many different kinds of families, the family is central to the lives of most of us. The families in this unit represent a variety of ethnic and socio-economic backgrounds. Some provide comfort and support; some generate conflict; one—perhaps the most troubling—exists only in a little girl's imagination. As you read these selections, consider the different ways in which families interact and even the different ways in which the term *family* can be defined.

My Family's Language

Richard Rodriguez

Looking Forward

The well-known writer and social commentator Richard Rodriguez began school knowing no more than fifty words of English. In this selection from his autobiography, *Hunger of Memory,* Rodriguez recalls that period in his boyhood in California when Spanish, the language of his Mexican immigrant parents and relatives, brought him comfort and security in the unfamiliar English-speaking world.

Help with Words

los gringos *(paragraph 2):* speakers of English (Spanish)
polysyllabic *(paragraph 4):* having several syllables
los otros *(paragraph 5):* the others; those unlike oneself (Spanish)
barrio *(paragraph 5):* a Spanish-speaking neighborhood
gradations *(paragraph 9):* degrees, levels, stages
warily *(paragraph 9):* cautiously

1   I grew up in a house where the only regular guests were my relations. For one day, enormous families of relatives would visit and there would be so many people that the noise and the bodies would spill out to the backyard and front porch. Then, for weeks, no one came by. (It was usually a salesman who rang the

doorbell.) Our house stood apart. A gaudy yellow in a row of white bungalows. We were the people with the noisy dog. The people who raised pigeons and chickens. We were the foreigners on the block. A few neighbors smiled and waved. We waved back. But no one in the family knew the names of the old couple who lived next door; until I was seven years old, I did not know the names of the kids who lived across the street.

In public, my father and mother spoke a hesitant, accented, not always grammatical English. And they would have to strain—their bodies tense—to catch the sense of what was rapidly said by *los gringos*. At home they spoke Spanish. The language of the Mexican past sounded in counterpoint to the English of public society. The words would come quickly, with ease. Conveyed through those sounds was the pleasing, soothing, consoling reminder of being at home.

During those years when I was first conscious of hearing, my mother and father addressed me only in Spanish; in Spanish I learned to reply. By contrast, English *(inglés),* rarely heard in the house, was the language I came to associate with *gringos*. I learned my first words of English overhearing my parents speak to strangers. At five years of age, I knew just enough English for my mother to trust me on errands to stores one block away. No more.

I was a listening child, careful to hear the very different sounds of Spanish and English. Wide-eyed with hearing, I'd listen to sounds more than words. First, there were English *(gringo)* sounds. So many words were still unknown that when the butcher or the lady at the drugstore said something to me, exotic polysyllabic sounds would bloom in the midst of the sentences. Often, the speech of people in public seemed to me very loud, booming with confidence. The man behind the counter would literally ask, "What can I do for you?" But by being so firm and so clear, the sound of his voice said that he was a *gringo;* he belonged in public society . . .

But then there was Spanish. *Español:* my family's language. *Español:* the language that seemed to me a private language. I'd hear strangers on the radio and in the Mexican Catholic church across town speaking in Spanish, but I couldn't really believe that Spanish was a public language, like English. Spanish speakers, rather, seemed related to me, for I sensed that we shared—

through our language—the experience of feeling apart from *los gringos*. It was thus a ghetto Spanish that I heard and spoke. Like those whose lives are bound by a barrio, I was reminded by Spanish of my separateness from *los otros, los gringos* in power. But more intensely than for most barrio children—because I did not live in a barrio—Spanish seemed to me the language of home. (Most days it was only at home that I'd hear it.) It became the language of joyful return.

6   A family member would say something to me and I would feel myself specially recognized. My parents would say something to me and I would feel embraced by the sounds of their words. Those sounds said: *I am speaking with ease in Spanish. I am addressing you in words I never use with* los gringos. *I recognize you as someone special, close, like no one outside. You belong with us. In the family.*

7   (Ricardo.)

8   At the age of five, six, well past the time when most other children no longer easily notice the difference between sounds uttered at home and words spoken in public, I had a different experience. I lived in a world magically compounded of sounds. I remained a child longer than most; I lingered too long, poised at the edge of language—often frightened by the sounds of *los gringos*, delighted by the sounds of Spanish at home. I shared with my family a language that was startlingly different from that used in the great city around us.

9   For me there were none of the gradations between public and private society so normal to a maturing child. Outside the house was public society; inside the house was private. Just opening or closing the screen door behind me was an important experience. I'd rarely leave home all alone or without reluctance. Walking down the sidewalk, under the canopy of tall trees, I'd warily notice the—suddenly—silent neighborhood kids who stood warily watching me. Nervously, I'd arrive at the grocery store to hear there the sounds of the *gringo*—foreign to me—reminding me that in this world so big, I was a foreigner. But then I'd return. Walking back toward our house, climbing the steps from the sidewalk, when the front door was open in summer, I'd hear voices beyond the screen door talking in Spanish. For a second or two, I'd stay, linger there, listening. Smiling, I'd hear my mother call out, saying in Spanish (words): "Is that you,

Richard?" All the while her sounds would assure me: *You are home now; come closer; inside. With us.*

"*Sí*," I'd reply.

Once more inside the house I would resume (assume) my place in the family. The sounds would dim, grow harder to hear. Once more at home, I would grow less aware of that fact. It required, however, no more than the blurt of the doorbell to alert me to listen to sounds all over again. The house would turn instantly still while my mother went to the door. I'd hear her hard English sounds. I'd wait to hear her voice return to soft-sounding Spanish, which assured me, as surely as did the clicking tongue of the lock on the door, that the stranger was gone.

A Second Look

1. To the young Rodriguez, what were the major differences between Spanish and English?

2. What does Rodriguez mean by "the gradations between public and private society so normal to a maturing child" (paragraph 9)? Why are there no such gradations in his childhood?

3. How does the author's use of concrete details help us understand the inside (private) and outside (public) worlds in which he grew up. Cite specific examples.

A Cyberlook

1. Richard Rodriguez has written and spoken much about his ancestry, but he is particularly interested in the Indian part of his Mexican heritage. It was in Mexico City, he remarks, that he first had his vision: "In the capital of Spanish colonialism there were Indian faces like mine everywhere. Where, then, was the conquistador?" To read Rodriguez's remarks on this subject, as well as others, such as bilingual education and affirmative action, see Paul Crowley, "An Ancient Catholic: An Interview with Richard Rodriguez." Access *InfoTrac College Edition* and search under the name of either the author or the subject.

2. In a TV essay entitled "A Cultural Identity" (18 June 1997), Richard Rodriguez discusses the subject of ethnic labels. He finds the label "Hispanic" to be almost meaningless because it confuses the classifications of race and culture. You will find the essay on the *Online Newshour* web site, maintained by PBS (the Public Broadcasting System). If you have difficulty finding the site, go to the *Wadsworth Developmental English* web page and click on Textbook Resource Centers.

Your instructor may ask the entire class to read this essay or ask a few to read it and report to the rest. If so, the class members may discuss whether they agree with Rodriguez or not. Are there other groups of "hyphenated Americans" whose labels are not as precise as they may at first seem. Do ethnic labels in general increase our sensitivity to diversity, or do they fragment the American population?

Ideas for Writing

1. If you have lived in a bilingual culture, describe your experiences with the two languages. Assume that your readers know one of the languages well, but not the other.

2. It is not just language that can make us feel like foreigners. We can be "others" in many settings. Write about an experience in which you felt like a stranger in someone else's culture. Be certain it is clear what your situation was and why you felt alien within it.

3. Richard Rodriguez has said that in spite of (or perhaps because of) his early experiences, he does not favor bilingual education. Write a paper in which you examine the pros and cons of this issue and show which side you support. (Information about bilingual education is available in your library and from *InfoTrac College Edition* or other Internet sources.)

Becoming Helpless

Colette Dowling

Looking Forward

This selection from Colette Dowling's book, *The Cinderella Complex*, explains some of the ways that women are taught dependence and submissiveness within their families at an early age. Dowling's father forcefully argued for her to accept his ideas and attitudes. Her mother was already dominated by the father's stronger personality. Dowling's self-examination leads her to believe that women are often actually afraid to succeed, a problem she calls the Cinderella complex.

Help with Words

metronome *(paragraph 1):* an instrument for marking time
chronic *(paragraph 1):* long-lasting
elusiveness *(paragraph 2):* the quality of being hard to know or understand
confrontation *(paragraph 2):* a face-to-face conflict
intimidated *(paragraph 2):* made timid
palpable *(paragraph 2):* easily seen
loomed *(paragraph 3):* appeared
didactic *(paragraph 3):* inclined to teach or lecture others
authoritarian *(paragraph 3):* domineering
impinged *(paragraph 3):* crowded in on
lavishing *(paragraph 3):* giving freely
exuded *(paragraph 4):* sent out
disdain *(paragraph 7):* scorn or contempt
digress *(paragraph 7):* to wander from the topic
infusing *(paragraph 7):* pouring into
fledgling *(paragraph 8):* inexperienced or early
ruddy *(paragraph 8):* healthy red

For many years I thought that my problems had to do with my father. Not until I was in my thirties did I begin to suspect that feelings about my mother were part of the inner conflict that had begun developing in me when I was very young. My mother was an even-tempered person, not given to screaming or fits of temper, always there, always waiting when my brother and I came home from school. She took me to dance lessons when I was very small, and later—until I was well into my teens—insisted that I practice the piano every day. She would sit by me and count, as regular and predictable as a metronome. Equally predictable was the afternoon nap she took, the small retreat from the reality of her daily life. She was given to illnesses of a chronic variety: headaches, bursitis, fatigue.

On the surface, there didn't seem to be anything so unusual about her life: she was the typical housewife/mother of her time. And yet . . . that peculiar elusiveness, and the little illnesses, so many of which, I think now (and so does she), were related to unexpressed anger. She avoided confrontation with my father and appeared to us children to be thoroughly intimidated by him. When she did speak out on some issue, the strain it caused her was palpable. She feared him.

In comparison with my mother, my father loomed large and vivid in my life—forceful Father with the big voice, big gestures, rude and sometimes embarrassing ways. He was didactic, authoritarian, and no one who knew him could easily dismiss him. Dislike, yes; there were certainly those who could summon forth that sentiment. But no one could pretend he wasn't there. He forced himself upon the consciousness of those with whom he came into contact; his personality impinged. You thought that he was lavishing attention upon you, but often the conversations seemed to spring more from some hidden need of his own.

I loved him. I adored the sureness he exuded, the idealism, the high, edgy energy. His laboratory in the engineering building at Johns Hopkins University was cool and impressive with its big, cold pieces of equipment. He was The Professor. My mother would refer to him, when speaking with others, as

"Dr. Hoppmann." She referred to herself as Mrs. Hoppmann. "Mrs. Hoppmann speaking," she would say, when answering the phone, as if to take refuge of some sort in the formality of the phrase, and in the use of my father's name. We were, in fact, a rather formal family.

In his work—which was his life—my father dealt with chalk, numbers, and steel. In his laboratory were machines. On his desk was a massive paperweight someone in the Metallurgy Department had given him, a hunk of smoothly ground steel with a cold, precisely cut cross at the top. I liked to heft the weight of it in my hand. I also wondered why anyone would ever admire it, as it was neither beautiful nor inspiring.

In the face of my father's demanding personality, my mother seemed to have difficulty holding her own. She was quiet and dutiful, a woman who'd grown up as the fourteenth of sixteen children in a Nebraska farm family. Somewhere along in her sixties, she started—quietly, determinedly—to live her own life, almost in spite of my father. My mother grew tougher and more interesting with age, but when I was growing up she was not tough at all; she was submissive. This same submissiveness was something I saw in virtually every woman I met, growing up—a need to defer to the man who was "taking care of" her, the man on whom she depended for everything.

By the time I entered high school I was bringing my ideas home from school—not to Mother, but to Father. There, at the dinner table, he would dissect them with passionate disdain. Then he would move on, digress, go off on a trip of his own that had little to do with me, but always infusing the conversation with great energy. His energy became my energy, or so I thought.

My father considered it his God-given duty to point me in the direction of truth—specifically, to correct the mistaken attitudes inflicted upon me by the "third-rate intellects" who were my teachers. His own role as teacher was more fascinating to him by far, I think now, than my fledgling development as a learner. At the age of twelve or thirteen I began to pursue what was to become a lifelong ambition: to get my father to shut up. It was a peculiar, mutual dependence that we had: I wanted his attention; he wanted mine. He believed that if I would only sit still and listen, he could hand me the world, whole and flawless, like a peeled pear on a silver plate. I didn't want to sit still, and I didn't want the peeled pear. I wanted to find life on my own, in my own way, to stumble upon it like a surprise in a field—the ruddy if misshapen apple that falls from an unpruned tree.

A Second Look

1. To explain how she gradually lost self-confidence and independence, Dowling describes the differing personalities of her mother and father. Describe in your own words the role model her mother provided.

2. Contrast Dowling's father and mother.

3. When did the conflict between Dowling and her father begin? Describe it.

4. Why, according to Dowling's father, did he force his ideas and attitudes on her? Why did she resent this?

5. A simile is a comparison usually signaled by the words *like* or *as*. In paragraph 8, Dowling uses two similes to explain how her father's attitudes differ from her own. In the first, the world is compared to a "peeled pear on a silver plate." In the second, life is compared to a "ruddy if misshapen apple." Contrast the two attitudes that these similes suggest.

6. In what ways might Dr. Hoppmann's profession have contributed to his personality and behavior?

A Cyberlook

1. In her 1998 book, *Maxing Out: Why Women Sabotage Their Financial Security*, Colette Dowling examines the financial disasters women sometimes suffer because they apparently believe if they become financially helpless, someone will come along and bail them out. The women whose problems Dowling examines include the author herself and Sarah, Duchess of York (Fergie). To learn more about this book and see whether you might be interested in reading it, see the review by Barbara Jacobs available on *InfoTrac College Edition*.

2. On 11 June 1998, Colette Dowling discussed *Maxing Out* and the subject of women's financial dependency on *Good Morning America*. See Clare Weiss, "Cinderella Makes a Comeback" on the ABC News web site. After reading Weiss's online article, click on Chat to read the comments of others who have experienced maxing out. If you have difficulty finding the site, go to the *Wadsworth Developmental English* web page and click on Textbook Resource Centers.

3. Many people (including college students) experience temporary difficulties with low checking accounts and/or high credit card debt. For some, however, impulse buying and indebtedness may be symptoms of a serious psychological problem. Working in small groups, discuss this topic: What are the warning signs of compulsive borrowing and spending? Then visit the Debtors Anonymous web site and click on Signposts on the Road to becoming a Compulsive Debtor. Compare your group lists with the results of DA's research.

Ideas for Writing

1. The title of Dowling's chapter, "Becoming Helpless," suggests that the author's purpose is to analyze the causes that brought about a particular effect, feelings of helplessness and dependency in later life.

Choose an important characteristic of your own personality. Are you shy, fearful, self-confident, studious, religious, and so on? Try to decide what people or places or situations made you the way you are. Make notes as you think about causes and effects in your life. Write down specific details.

You could organize your essay by first describing a particular characteristic. How does it show up in your personality? What difference does it make in your life? Then, in the body of the paper, explain what caused this to be a characteristic of your personality. Describe the cause or causes in detail.

2. Do you feel that women now in their late teens or early twenties are less likely to become helpless than those of Dowling's generation? Has Cinderella learned to depend more on herself and less on the Prince? Is the Prince's attitude still part of the problem? Based on your own thinking and that of your friends, write a paper in which you examine this issue. Use specific examples to support your point of view.

The Great Sisters and Brothers War

Andrew Shanley

Looking Forward

Andrew Shanley explains that conflict among the children in a family, sibling rivalry, is nearly unavoidable. The fighting can be intense and disturbing, but it usually passes with childhood.

Help with Words

writhing *(paragraph 2)*: twisting
ensuing *(paragraph 3)*: following
cowering *(paragraph 4)*: crouching in fear
impassioned *(paragraph 4)*: filled with emotion
glowering *(paragraph 7)*: looking with anger
banished *(paragraph 11)*: made to go
dastardly *(paragraph 11)*: mean
dissuade *(paragraph 13)*: persuade not to do something

The evening had been going especially well. As we often do when entertaining guests with children, we fed the kids first so that the adults could have a quiet dinner. All major events in our lives had just about been covered when our friends' two boys and our two stormed into the dining room, announced that it was time for dessert, then raced into the kitchen.

I was clearing the dishes when we heard a crash, followed by a child's howl. We got to the kitchen in time to see our friends' seven-year-old, Kevin, writhing on the floor and bellowing about killing his brother, Tod, nine.

Physical damage was minimal, but mental anguish was considerable. Apparently there had been an argument over who would scoop the ice cream. In the ensuing scuffle, Tod had pushed Kevin to the floor.

Now Tod stood cowering in the corner. His mother was giving him an impassioned lecture.

"Don't you realize that if you can't get along with your own flesh and blood you can't get along with anybody?" she was asking. "Don't you understand that nobody in the world loves you more than your brother? And this is how you treat him!"

Tod kept his eyes focused on the floor, no doubt wishing he could be transported to another planet.

I looked at Kevin, who was wiping tears from his cheeks and glowering at his brother like a boxer before the bell signaling the start of the next round. His father was leaning over and speaking softly to him.

"I'm sure Tod didn't mean it, Kev," he said. "He just got excited about the ice cream, that's all. The last thing he'd want to do is hurt you."

I wanted Kevin to answer, "Come off it, Dad; he wanted to knock my head off and you know it!" I was certain I'd smile and cheer if he did, so I hurried away before his reply.

Did our friends really think that siblings should have total control over their emotions and aggressions? If only Tod's mother had acknowledged how easy it is to fight with a brother or sister, then explained it was up to him, the older brother, to show restraint.

As I wiped the dining room table, I thought about my brother, my sister and I as we were growing up. To call what we experienced sibling rivalry is an understatement; it was more like the Great Brothers and Sisters War. I remembered the time my brother and I locked our sister in the closet and "lost" the key—and the time she hit me with the croquet mallet and fractured my finger. We were all regulars in solitary—our bedrooms—where we were banished in an effort to break our urge to commit such dastardly deeds upon one another.

We were by no means oddballs among our peer group, either. One friend of mine stuck such a big wad of gum in his sister's beloved shoulder-length hair that it had to be clipped back to her ears. I'm sure she got her revenge, too, though I can't recall how. These wars were never-ending.

Siblings know each other's most sensitive buttons as well as when to push them for maximum outrage. Our parents tried every way possible to dissuade us from doing battle, but never told us that fighting with a brother or sister was monstrous and abnormal behavior. Instead, they acknowledged that living together peacefully was difficult, and this was all the more reason to work at it.

"You'd better learn to get along," I can hear my mother telling the three of us as if it were yesterday, "because there will be times when all you'll have is each other."

I think we somehow understood. Even on those days when we were nastiest to one another, when we swore our grudges would last into eternity, we'd still climb into our beds and talk long after the lights were out. In time, the three of us became the best of friends. In fact, my brother and I each stood as best man at the other's wedding.

As parents, we hate to see our children fight. We often feel the blows as if they had landed on us; it hurts to see those we love go against each other. That's natural. But it's important to recognize that problems between sisters and brothers can be part of their competition for our love and attention. And when difficulties do arise, we should make an extra effort to demonstrate our love for them all, possibly focusing it where most needed at that particular moment.

When two young boys are diving for the ice cream, however, it's every man for himself with no regard for bloodlines. Later that evening, Tod was playing with our dog when he fell backward over a coffee table onto the floor. He shouted for help. I watched as Kevin ran over and looked down at his brother wedged between the overturned table and the couch.

"Got yourself in a bit of a fix, big brother, haven't you?" Kevin asked, smiling and enjoying the moment. Then he reached over to offer Tod a hand. "You owe me," he said, as he pulled the older boy to his feet. "I could have gotten you good."

The Great Brothers and Sisters War is often troubling, but as with most wars, it has its own codes, as well as its own cycles. And when the bell sounds for the final round—the one that really counts—our kids usually come out and shake hands. 19

A Second Look

1. As many writers do, Shanley captures our attention with an illustration before he states the main idea of his essay. What is his main idea, and in which paragraph do you find it?

2. Shanley's sentences often state his ideas with no wasted words. For these economical sentences to work well, they must be carefully structured. What are the patterns of the second sentence in paragraph 1 and the first sentence in paragraph 3?

3. In paragraph 7, Kevin is compared to a boxer, and in paragraphs 11 and 12 the conflicts between brothers and sisters are described as wars. The essay ends with another reference to boxing. Why does Shanley use this exaggeration?

4. The essay ends by returning to Kevin and Tod. Is the dialogue between the two boys in paragraph 18 true to life? Is this what the boys are likely to have said to each other? Why or why not?

A Cyberlook

Andrew Shanley's look at the "war" among siblings is lighthearted, and his conclusion is positive. Sometimes, however, these wars leave casualties. In a recent study of over 200 college students, psychologist Carol Wilson found that many had suffered physical or verbal abuse from siblings. She found that the responses of the objects of such abuse varied according to gender and that there were dramatic differences between short-term and long-term effects. Wilson's study was reported in *Jet*. You can access it on *InfoTrac College Edition* by searching the periodical entries under "sibling rivalry." For other studies and articles on the topic, search "sibling rivalry" using your web browser.

Ideas for Writing

One way to describe the organization of Shanley's essay is to say that it defines the term *sibling rivalry*. The author uses a detailed illustration and several other examples to explain what sibling rivalry is. He also discusses the characteristics of the rivalry and compares it to fighting and war to make it clear.

Choose a term that you understand thoroughly. It might be a term such as *peer pressure, discrimination, significant other, extra effort,* or *inferiority complex*. Write an essay in which you try to make the term clear to the reader by giving illustrations of it. What might you compare it to? What does it differ from? Make the term as clear and understandable as possible. Anyone could look up the word in a dictionary, but knowledge from experience will make the term truly understandable. Look at the essays by Jason Flanary, David Raymond, Pete Axthelm, and Marjorie Franco to see how other writers have developed essays using definition.

Mrs. Razor

James Still

Looking Forward

In James Still's short story, Elvy, a six-year-old girl growing up in rural Appalachia, creates an imaginary family that begins to take over her real world. Her pretend family causes increasing distress in her true one.

Help with Words

gilly trees *(paragraph 1):* Balm of Gilead trees, a variety of poplar
Cincinnati stove *(paragraph 1):* a wood-burning stove for heating and cooking
lazy shuck *(paragraph 2):* a no-good, a do-nothing
mite *(paragraph 2):* a bit, a tiny amount
diddles *(paragraph 3):* baby chicks
victuals *(paragraph 4):* food (pronounced, and sometimes incorrectly spelled, *vittles*)
Old Scratch *(paragraph 4):* Satan
keened his eyes *(paragraph 11):* focused narrowly, looked hard at
day-eye blossoms *(paragraph 20):* daisies
lawed *(paragraph 21):* brought before the law, arrested
gallus *(paragraph 23):* suspenders (usually plural, *galluses*)

"We'll have to do something about that child," Father said. We sat in the kitchen eating our supper, though day still held and the chickens had not yet gone to roost in the gilly trees. Elvy was crying behind the stove, and her throat was raw with sobbing. Morg and I paused, bread in hand, and glanced over our shoulder. The firebox of the Cincinnati stove winked, the iron flowers of the oven throbbed with heat. Mother tipped a finger to her lips, motioning Father to hush. Father's voice lifted, "I figure a small thrashing would make her leave off this foolish notion."

Elvy was six years old. She was married, to hear her tell it, and had three children and a lazy shuck of a husband who cared not a mite for his own and left his family to live upon her kin. The thought had grown into truth in her mind. I could play at being Brother Hemp Leckett, climb onto a chopblock and preach to the fowls; or I could be Round George Parks, riding the creeks, killing all who crossed my path; I could be any man body. Morg couldn't make-believe; he was just Morg. But Elvy had imagined herself old and thrown away by a husband, and she kept believing.

"A day will come," Elvy told us, "when my man's going to get killed down dead, the way he's living." She spoke hard of her husband and was a shrew of a wife who thought only of her children; she was as busy with her young as a hen with diddles. It was a dog's life she led, washing rags of clothes, sewing with a straw for needle, singing by the half hour to cradled arms, and keeping an eye sharp for gypsies. She jerked at loose garments and fastened and pinned, as Mother did to us.

Once we spied her in the grape arbor making to put a jacket on a baby that wouldn't hold still. She slapped the air, saying, "Hold up, young'un!" Morg stared, half believing. Later she claimed her children were stolen. It wasn't by the dark people. Her husband had taken them—she didn't know where. For days she sat pale and small, minced her victuals, and fretted in her sleep. She had wept, "My man's the meanest critter ever was. Old Scratch is bound to get him."

And now Elvy's husband was dead. She had run to Mother to tell this thing, the news having come in an unknown way. She waited dry-eyed and shocked until Father rode in from the fields in middle afternoon and she met him at the barn gate to choke out her loss.

"We've got to haste to Biggety Creek and fetch my young'uns ere the gypsies come," she grieved. "They're left alone."

"Is he doornail dead?" Father had asked. And he smiled to hear Biggety Creek named, the Nowhere Place he had told us of once at table. Biggety Creek where heads are the size of water buckets, where noses are turned up like old shoes, women wear skillets for hats, and men screw their breeches on, and where people are so proper they eat with little fingers pointing, and one pea at a time. Father rarely missed a chance to preach us a sermon.

"We've got to haste," Elvy pled.

"Do you know the road to Biggety Creek?"

Elvy nodded.

Father keened his eyes to see what manner of child was his own, his face lengthening and his patience wearing thin. He grabbed his hat off and clapped it angrily against his leg; he strode into the barn, fed the mules, and came to the house with Elvy tagging after and weeping.

"Fix an early supper," he told Mother.

Father's jaws were set as he drew his chair to the table. The day was still so bright the wall bore a shadow of the unkindled lamp. Elvy had hidden behind the stove, lying on the cat's pallet, crying. "Come and eat your victuals," Mother begged, for her idea was to humor children and let them grow out of their notions. But Elvy would not.

We knew Father's hand itched for a hickory switch. Disobedience angered him quicker than anything. Yet he only looked worried. The summer long he had teased Elvy, trying to shake her belief. Once while shaving he had asked, "What ever made you marry a lump of a husband who won't come home, never furnishes a cent?" Morg and I stood by to spread left-over lather on our faces and scrape it off with a kitchen knife. "I say it's past strange I've not met my own son-in-law. I hunger to shake his hand and welcome him to the family, ask him to sit down to our board and stick his feet under."

Father had glanced slyly at Elvy. "What's his name? Upon my honor, I haven't been told."

Elvy looked up. Her eyes glazed in thought. "He's called Razor."

"Given name or family?"

"Just Razor."

"Ask him to visit us," Father urged in mock seriousness. "Invite him up for Sunday dinner."

Elvy had promised that her husband would come. She had Mother fry a chicken, the dish he liked best, claiming the gizzard was his chosen morsel. Nothing less than the flax tablecloth was good enough, and she gathered day-eye blossoms for the centerpiece. An extra chair was placed, and we waited; we waited noon through, until one o'clock. Then she told us confidentially, "Go ahead and eat. Razor allus was slow as Jim Christmas."

She carried a bowl of soup behind the Cincinnati stove to feed her children. In the evening she explained, "I've learnt why my man stayed away. He hain't got a red cent to his pocket and he's scared of being lawed for not supporting his young'uns."

Father had replied, "I need help—need a workhand to grub corn ground. A dollar a day I'll pay, greenback on the barrel top. I want a feller with lard in his elbows and willing to work. Fighting sourwood sprouts is like going to war. If Razor has got the measure of the job, I'll hire him and promise not to law."

"I ought never to a-took him for a husband," Elvy confessed. "When first I married he was smart as ants. Now he's turned so lazy he won't even fasten his gallus buckles. He's slouchy and no 'count."

"Humn," Father had grunted, eyeing Morg and me, the way our clothes hung on us. "Sloth works on a feller," he preached. "It grows roots. He'll start letting his sleeves flare and shirttail go hang. One day he gets too sorry to bend and lace his shoes, and it's a *swarp, swarp* every step. A time comes he'll not latch the top button of his breeches—ah, when a man turns his potty out, he's beyond cure."

"That's Razor all over," Elvy had said.

Father's teasing had done no good. As we sat at supper that late afternoon, listening to Elvy sob behind the stove, Morg began to stare into his plate and would eat no more. He believed Elvy. Tears hung on his chin.

Father's face tightened, half in anger, half in dismay. He lifted his hands in defeat. "Hell's bangers!" he blurted. Morg's tears fell thicker. I spoke small into his ear, "Act it's not so," but Morg could never makelike.

Father suddenly thrust back his chair. "Hurry and get ready," he ordered, "the whole push of you. We're going to Biggety Creek." His voice was dry as a stick.

Elvy's sobbing hushed. Morg blinked. The room became so quiet I could hear flames eating wood in the firebox. Father arose and made long-legged strides toward the barn to harness the mules.

We mounted the wagon, Father and Mother to the spring seat, Elvy settling between; I stood with Morg behind the seat. Dusk was creeping out of the hollows. Chickens walked toward the gilly trees, flew to their roosts, sleepy and quarrelsome. Father gathered the reins and angled the whip to start the mules. "Now, which way?" he asked Elvy. She pointed ahead and we rode off.

The light faded. Night came. The shapes of trees and fences were lost and there were only the wise eyes of the mules to pick the road when the ground had melted and the sky was gone. Elvy nodded fitfully, trying to keep awake. We traveled six miles before Father turned back.

A Second Look

1. What are the major differences among the three children—Elvy, Morg, and the narrator?

2. How does Still use both direct and indirect description to show his readers Father's complex reactions to Elvy's worsening problem?

3. Is this story is completely open ended, or does Still suggest what direction the action might take next?

Ideas for Writing

1. If you or someone you know had a very "real" imaginary childhood companion, describe that experience. How did the child finally leave the imaginary relationship behind. Be sure to show your readers what all the participants—real and imaginary—are like.

2. Using your library or on-line references, write a brief report on delusional behavior. Note that such behavior has different types, causes, symptoms, and treatments. If your instructor asks you to document your paper, you may consult a handbook or get on-line help from the *Purdue On-Line Writing Lab* (OWL). Search for "MLA citation" or click on Resources for Writers.

Two Dads Are Better Than One?

Angela Waugh

Looking Forward

In this essay written for a freshman composition class, Angela Waugh contrasts her stepfather with her biological father in order to decide which she should care about more. She hopes that looking at their differences will help her decide what her relationship with them should be.

Help with Words

necessities *(paragraph 1):* basic needs
elders *(paragraph 5):* people who are older
objectively *(paragraph 8):* fairly
obligated *(paragraph 9):* bound by a sense of duty

I've always envied people with only two parents. They never have to feel sorry for their real father because he is lonely, and they never have to feel they should care more about their stepfather because he is the one who has provided them with the necessities most of their lives.

I, since I have two fathers, have known these feelings. I know what it's like trying to decide which father I should care about more so that I could tell my friends the next time they asked.

3   It really should be a clear-cut decision. My two fathers are so different in everything that I should be able to look at these differences and decide.

4   A major difference between the two is how responsible they are. My stepfather has always had a steady job. He enjoys going to work each day and knowing that at the end of the week he'll get a paycheck. With this paycheck he pays bills, buys groceries, and makes sure we all have clothes to wear. On the other hand, my father doesn't particularly care for steady jobs. He is a singer and has worked three or four nights a week in nightclubs most of his life. With his money, he buys things like new guitars and amplifiers. His idea of providing for us, as Mom tells me, is to send ten dollars a month, which is to be divided three ways. He only does this, however, when he's out of state.

5   Discipline is another major difference between my two fathers. My stepfather, who can be very strict at times, believes that children should obey their parents, do what they are told when they are told to do it, and respect their elders. My father, who was never disciplined himself, has quite different views. He has always encouraged my brothers and me to rebel against rules, to ask why we had to do certain things, and to resent being made to do things we thought were stupid. (Going to bed at ten was stupid.) My mother always told us that our father only did this to cause trouble, but I'm not so sure about that. Maybe he did, but then again maybe he thought going to bed at ten was stupid, too!

6   Education is another big issue my stepfather is concerned about. He believes, like many people, that to be able to succeed in life, one has to have a good education. He always told us that he didn't want us to turn out like he did, a truck driver who had to be away from his family for weeks at a time. He used to punish me and my brothers for making C's on our report cards. His theory is that a C is average, and his kids are not average. I wouldn't place any money on that.

7   My father believes that an education is good to have, but one doesn't have to have it to survive. He always says, "Look at me; I made it." I don't think, however, that I would call sleeping in the back of a station wagon "making it!"

8   So here I have it. All their differences down on paper, and I can look at them objectively and decide which father to love more—but it isn't that easy.

I love my father because he is just that, my natural father. I respect him; I am obligated to him, and I want to make him proud of me. Then there is my stepfather, whom I respect very much; whom I feel obligated to; whom I want to make proud of me; and, most important of all, whom I have grown to love as much as any child could possibly love a parent.

I guess I'll never really know which father I love more. I don't see why I should have to love either more. I think I'll just love both of them in almost equal amounts.

A Second Look

1. Look again at paragraphs 4–7. Write down a word or phrase that states the main idea of each of these paragraphs. Now check to see what specific information Waugh uses to develop each of these topics.

2. In paragraph 4, what phrase helps Waugh unify her discussion of her two fathers? Are there words, phrases, or sentences that link ideas in other paragraphs?

3. Does Waugh's essay suggest an answer to the question asked by the title?

4. Why do you think Waugh cannot choose between her fathers?

Ideas for Writing

Do you know two people who are somewhat alike but also different? They might be two friends, two relatives, two teachers, or two roommates. Pick two such people, and write an essay showing specifically how they are different.

Begin with one or two paragraphs that introduce your two subjects to the reader. The body of your paper will focus on the differences. Use at least one paragraph to develop each major point with facts, examples, or other supporting details.

Up the Hill

Ryan Hardesty

Looking Forward

Traditions bond families together, bringing present members closer and linking them with the generations that came before them. Not all these traditions are happy ones, but even the sad ones may give families a sense of unity. In this student essay, Ryan Hardesty describes how generations of his family have said farewell to their dead.

Help with Words

treacherous *(paragraph 1):* risky, dangerous
clad *(paragraph 9):* dressed
eerie *(paragraph 9):* strange, ghostly

The black jeep roared into life and began its treacherous journey up the steep, muddy road that led to our family cemetery at the top of the hill. I could see Uncle Jim's bald head near the back window, and beside him sat my weeping mother, her hands over her eyes. I couldn't make out any of the other people from this distance, though I knew they were all relatives, riding up the hill for my grandmother's funeral. I watched the jeep for several seconds, until it turned a corner and disappeared behind a clump of pines.

"Come on, boy," my grandfather said, placing his broad, weathered hand on my shoulder. "Let's go up and say goodbye to your Grandma." I grabbed his hand and we began the long climb to the cemetery. We had gone only a few yards along the narrow, muddy road when I began my usual stream of questions.

"Why didn't we ride up, Grandpa?" I asked, staring up into his wrinkled face.

"It didn't seem proper," he answered. He paused for a moment, leaning against an old elm tree. I could tell he was tired because he was breathing hard. "Ever since I was a little boy, we carried our people up this mountain. Somehow it don't seem right to take somebody up in a truck. They ought to be carried, the way 'most everybody up there was carried, by the people who cared the most. It seems to me that's the least you can do for a person who's gone."

We started walking again, our feet crunching through the thick covering of dead leaves and sinking into the mud beneath them. It became steeper here, just above the old elm tree, and I had to struggle to keep moving. I wondered how Grandpa could walk so fast as old as he was. Maybe he was just used to it.

"I've walked this old road many times," Grandpa said, as if he'd read my thoughts, "and it never gets any easier." We paused for a few minutes. He pulled a ragged yellow handkerchief from his coat pocket and wiped his forehead. "You know how we used to take people up?" he asked, cramming the handkerchief back into his pocket.

"No," I lied, "how did you take people up?"

"We had to carry them, casket and all, clear to the top. It took eight, sometimes ten men to carry somebody up this muletrail, and it was even worse in those days. We didn't have none of this ridin' up in trucks and such. We used our own strength to carry our loved ones home."

He sounded as though he were finished, so I started walking, using the branch I had snapped from the elm as a walking stick. We were almost at the top now, and I could see the black jeep sitting on the hillside, its knobby tires deep in the mud. I could see the grandfather oak standing by the gate, guarding the entrance to the cemetery. I could see my darkly clad family standing in a circle, praying softly. And I could see the shiny black casket sitting on the ground. Suddenly, everyone began singing, filling the cold air with an eerie, mournful sound that caused my knees to tremble and my skin to crawl.

"Did you carry up a lot of people, Grandpa?" I asked, needing the reassurance of my voice to drown out the fear.

"I sure did," he said. He wiped his forehead again, only this time he used the back of his hand. "I helped carry up my papa, right after I got married. It was a day almost like today, only colder. I remember we slipped in the mud and almost let him slide over the hill. My two uncles brought Momma up that day, chair and all, because she was sick and couldn't walk on her own. A few months later I helped carry up Momma, only this time she didn't need the chair. I helped carry up your Grandma's mother, two uncles, and a few good friends." His voice sounded funny now, and I realized he was crying. I walked on ahead and stood beside the grandfather oak, watching as they lowered Grandma into the cold, damp ground. Everyone was crying, and I think maybe I cried a little too. Then it was over and time to go home.

As I walked back down, I started thinking about Grandpa. He had carried people up this hill lots of times. It must have hurt as he watched his friends and family die and be carried up the hill. I wondered if he thought about the day when he would be carried up, and if he was afraid. Then I thought about myself, a grown man, carrying Momma up the hill like that. And I saw myself . . .

I ran all the way down, my eyes filled with tears and my clothes covered with mud. I caught up with Grandpa, grabbed his hand, and let him brush away my tears.

I'll hold your hand, Grandpa, I thought, until it's your turn to go. Then, if I'm lucky, somebody will hold my hand until it's my turn. And I want them to carry me up. None of this riding up in trucks and such.

A Second Look

1. Hardesty uses a setting that may not be familiar to many readers. Pick out some of the details that help us get a clear picture of the location.

2. Writers often use dialogue to suggest (rather than directly state) something about the people they are describing. What does the old man's speech tell readers about him? Does his speech sound realistic?

3. What is the grandfather's attitude about transporting the dead to the cemetery? Why does he feel this way?

4. What details in the essay indicate that this family tradition will be carried on by the next generation?

Ideas for Writing

Write about a tradition in your own family. Besides burial customs, there are many traditions: celebrating holidays, observing birthdays, holding weddings, going to reunions, and so forth. You might describe how such a tradition is carried out over time—for example, telling your readers how your family celebrates Christmas year after year or how they gather annually for grandfather's birthday. On the other hand, you might focus on one particular occasion—a particular Thanksgiving dinner, a specific Seder, the 1998 family reunion held on the Fourth of July, your sixteenth birthday party—that will provide a concrete example of how the tradition is observed.

Making Connections

1. The essays of Colette Dowling and Angela Waugh and the short story by James Still all focus on the relationships of fathers and daughters. How are the fathers different in their actions and attitudes? Can you find any similarities among them? How have they influenced their daughters?

2. If you read Victoria Chen's "Chinese American Women, Language, and Moving Subjectivity" on *InfoTrac College Edition,* comment on the different attitudes of Maxine Hong Kingston and Richard Rodriguez toward their experiences growing up in a bilingual culture.

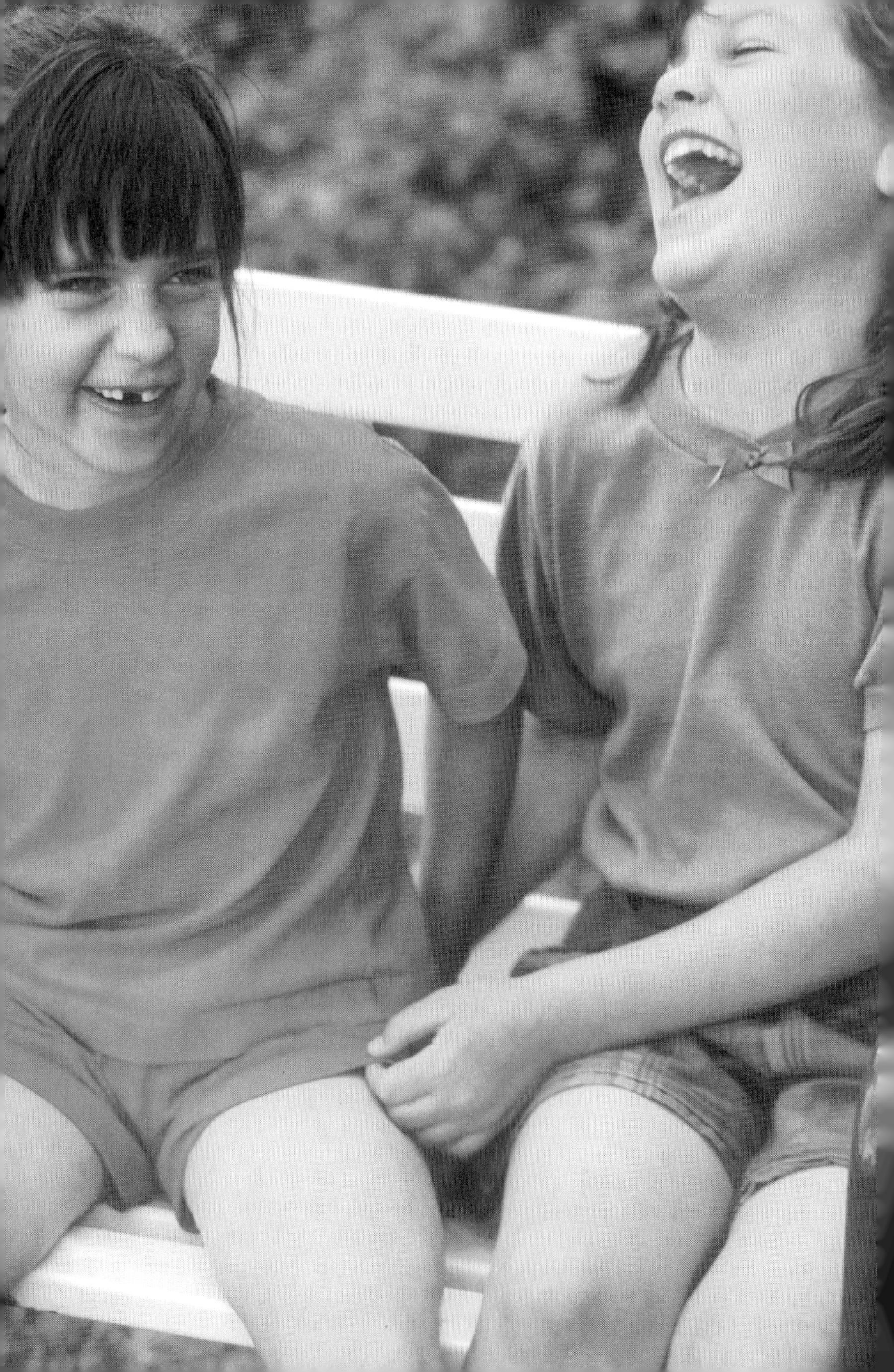

Laughter

The essays in this unit are held together not by a major idea, but by the fact that all were written to amuse readers. Though you may not be asked to write a humorous essay in your composition class, using the techniques of humor can often add life and interest to an essay on a fairly serious subject. In fact, some of the selections in this unit have a serious undercurrent. Observe carefully the techniques these writers use. Writing humorously is not necessarily easy, but it can be great fun.

After a Fall

Garrison Keillor

Looking Forward

Laughing at a fall in which no one is hurt is a typical reaction. Garrison Keillor, well-known writer, comedian, and radio host, admits that laughing is a natural response, but he then goes on to examine the feelings of the person who has fallen. The victim is likely to view the fall differently. Notice the carefully chosen words that help the reader see the actions Keillor describes.

Help with Words

adrenaline *(paragraph 1):* a hormone produced especially in frightening situations
prone *(paragraph 1):* inclined, likely to experience
inexplicable *(paragraph 1):* not explainable
smirk *(paragraph 3):* a knowing smile
rigorous *(paragraph 3):* demanding
artifacts *(paragraph 3):* man-made objects or tools
perspective *(paragraph 4):* a way of looking at a subject
fundamentalist *(paragraph 14):* holding religious beliefs based on a literal interpretation of the Bible
constricted *(paragraph 14):* limited
inevitable *(paragraph 14):* unavoidable
nonchalant *(paragraph 15):* unconcerned
venture *(paragraph 18):* undertaking, experience

When you happen to step off an edge you didn't see and lurch forward into space waving your arms, it's the end of the world for a second or two, and after you do land, even if you know you're O.K. and no bones are broken it may take a few seconds to decide whether this is funny or not. Your body is still worked up about the fall—especially the nervous system and the adrenaline-producing areas. In fact, I am still a little shaky from a spill that occurred two hours ago, when I put on a jacket, walked out the front door of this house here in St. Paul, Minnesota, and for no reason whatever took a plunge down five steps and landed on the sidewalk flat on my back with my legs up in the air. I am thirty-nine years old and in fairly good shape, not prone to blackouts or sudden dizziness, and so a sudden inexplicable fall comes as a big surprise to me.

A woman who was jogging down the street—a short, muscular young woman in a gray sweatshirt and sweatpants—stopped and asked if I was O.K. "Yeah! Fine!" I said and got right up. "I just fell, I guess," I said. "Thanks," I said. She smiled and trotted away.

Her smile has followed me into the house, and I see it now as a smirk, which is what it was. She was too polite to bend over and hoot and shriek and guffaw and cackle and cough and whoop and wheeze and slap her thighs and stomp on the ground, but it was there in that smile: a young woman who through rigorous physical training and feminist thinking has gradually been taking charge of her own life and ridding her attic of self-hatred and doubt and fear and mindless competitiveness and other artifacts of male-dominated culture is rewarded with the sight of a middle-aged man in a brown suit with a striped tie falling down some steps as if someone had kicked him in the pants.

I'm sorry if I don't consider this humorous. I would like to. I wish she had come over and helped me up and then perhaps sat on the steps with me while I calmed down. We might have got to talking about the fall and how each of us viewed it from a different perspective. . . .

I might have seen it her way, but she ran down the street, and now I can only see my side of the fall. I feel old and achy and ridiculous and cheapened by the whole experience. I understand now why my son was so angry with me a few months ago when he tripped on a shoelace and fell in the neighbor's yard—a yard where the neighbor's sheepdog had lived for years—and I cackled at him.

"It's not funny!" he yelled.

"Oh, don't be so sensitive," I said.

Don't be so sensitive! What a dumb thing to say! Who has the right to tell someone else how to feel? It is the right of the person who falls in the dog droppings to decide for himself or herself how he or she will feel. It's not up to a jury. The fallen person determines whether it's funny or not. . . .

Five years ago, I got on a bus with five musicians and rode around for two weeks doing shows every night. They played music; I told jokes and sang a song. One night, in the cafeteria of a junior college in southern Minnesota, we happened to draw a big crowd, and the stage—four big plywood sheets on three-foot steel legs—was moved back twenty feet to make room for more chairs. The show was late starting, the room was stuffy, the crowd was impatient, and when finally the lights dimmed and the spotlight shone on the plywood, I broke from the back door and made a run for the stage, thinking to make a dramatic entrance and give these fine people the show they were waiting for.

What I could not see in the dark was the ceiling and a low concrete overhang that the stage had been moved partly under, and then the spotlight caught me straight in the eyes and I couldn't see anything. I leaped up onto the stage, and in mid-leap my head hit concrete and my right leg caught the plywood at mid-shin. I toppled forward, stuck out my hands, and landed on my hands and knees. The crowd drew a long breath. I got right up—I had been doing shows long enough to know not to lie onstage and cry in front of a paying audience—and, seeing the microphone about ten feet ahead, strode up to it and held out my arms and said, "Hello everybody! I'm happy to be here!"

Then they laughed—a big thunderstorm of a laugh and a big round of applause for what they now saw had been a wonderful trick. But it wasn't funny! My neck hurt! I hurt all over! On the other hand, to see a tall man in a white suit jump directly into a ceiling and then fall down—how often does a person get to see that? Men dive off high towers through fiery hoops into tiny tanks, men rev up motorcycles and leap long rows of trucks and buses, but I am the only man in show business who takes a good run and jumps Straight Up Into Solid Concrete Using Only His Bare Head. Amazing! . . .

Oh, it is a sad story, except for the fact that it isn't. My ceiling jump got the show off to a great start. The band played three fast tunes, and I jumped carefully back onstage and did a monologue that the audience, which now knew I was funny, laughed at a lot. Even I, who had a headache, thought it was funny. I really did feel lucky.

So do I still—a tall man who fell now sitting down to write his memoirs. The body is so delicate, the skeleton so skinny; we are stick men pencilled in lightly, with a wooden stick cage to protect the heart and lungs and a cap of bone over the brain. I wonder that I have survived so many plunges, so many quick drops down the short arc that leads to the ground. . . .

The first time I ever went naked in mixed company was at the house of a girl whose father had a bad back and had built himself a sauna in the corner of the basement. Donna and I were friends in college. Both of us had grown up in fundamentalist Christian homes, and we liked to compare notes on that. We both felt constricted by our upbringings and were intent on liberating ourselves and becoming more free and open and natural. So it seemed natural and inevitable one night to wind up at her house with some of her friends there and her parents gone and to take off our clothes and have a sauna.

We were nineteen years old and were very cool ("Take off my clothes? Well, sure. Heck, I've taken them off dozens of times.") and were careful to keep cool and be nonchalant and not look at anybody below the neck. We got into the sauna as if getting on the bus. People do this, I thought to myself. There is nothing unusual about it! Nothing! We all have bodies! There is no reason to get excited! This is a normal part of life!

We filed into the little wooden room, all six of us, avoiding unnecessary body contact, and Donna poured a bucket of water on the hot rocks to make steam. It was very quiet. "There's a shower there on the wall if you want to take a shower," she said in a strange, nervous voice.

"Hey! How about a shower!" a guy said in a cool-guy voice, and he turned on the water full blast. The shower head leaped from the wall. It was a hand-held type—a nozzle at the end of a hose—and it jumped out at us like a snake and thrashed around exploding ice-cold water. He fell back, someone screamed, I slipped and fell, Donna fell on top of me, we leaped apart, and meanwhile the nozzle danced and flew from the force of the blast of water. Donna ran out of the sauna and slipped and fell on the laundry-room floor, and another girl yelled, "God damn you, Tom!" Donna scrambled to her feet. "God! Oh, God!" she cried. Tom yelled, "I'm sorry!" Another guy laughed a loud, wicked laugh, and I tiptoed out as fast as I could move, grabbed my clothes, and got dressed. Donna grabbed her clothes. "Are you all right?" I said, not looking at her or anything. "No!" she said. Somebody laughed a warm, appreciative laugh from inside the sauna. "Don't laugh!" she yelled. "It isn't funny! It isn't the least bit funny!"

"I'm not laughing," I said, though it wasn't me she was angry at. I still am not laughing. I think it's a very serious matter, twenty years later. Your first venture as a naked person, you want it to go right and be a good experience, and then some joker has to go pull a fast one. . . . 18

I haven't seen you since that night, Donna. I've told the sauna story to dozens of people over the years, and they all thought it was funny but I still don't know what you think. Are you all right? 19

A Second Look

1. Keillor opens the essay with a personal experience. In what paragraph does he state the main idea of the essay? What is it?

2. What does Keillor mean when he says in paragraph 3 that the woman's smile "followed me into the house"?

3. In paragraph 3, Keillor chooses unusual verbs to describe the way he imagines the woman would like to laugh at him. Explain why the description is amusing.

4. Look carefully at the way Keillor tells about his experience in the sauna. Describe some of the techniques that make the story amusing.

5. Why does Keillor end the essay with a question addressed to Donna? Why does he ask this particular question?

A Cyberlook

Many people know Garrison Keillor best from his long-running radio show on public radio, "A Prairie Home Companion," which celebrated its twenty-fifth anniversary in 1999. In recent years, Keillor has also written several books, released several sound recordings, and edited *The Best American Short Stories 1998*. To learn more about this multi-talented man, search his name using *InfoTrac College Edition* or any browser.

Ideas for Writing

1. Most people could add to Garrison Keillor's essay examples of funny or embarrassing falls they have had. In a paragraph or two, tell about some spill you have taken. Explain how it happened and what you looked like. Work especially on using detailed description that will help the reader imagine the actions. The test for success in this paper is whether the reader can see what you describe.

2. Victims of falls are like victims of jokes: They are expected to laugh at themselves and think no more about it. Have you ever been the butt of a joke that was funny to everyone except you? Write an essay in which you describe the joke and then explain your reaction to it. Try to make the reader understand your side of the story.

Pranks for the Memory

Dave Barry

Looking Forward

In his regular columns for the *Miami Herald*, humorist Dave Barry likes to look at the slightly (or sometimes very) ridiculous side of life. In this essay, Barry describes some amusing—and most "unscary"—traditions associated with Halloween. Some are new to the 1990s; others go back at least as far as Barry's boyhood.

Help with Words

confronted *(paragraph 4):* faced
inedible *(paragraph 8):* not eatable
Druid *(paragraph 10):* member of a Celtic order of priests, soothsayers, judges, and others in pre-Christian Britain, Ireland, and France
Stonehenge *(paragraph 10):* an ancient British structure built of huge free-standing stones (some weighing 30 tons), at one time associated with the Druids

I love Halloween. And not just because it gives us a chance to buy a new mailbox. No, what I love most is the fun of opening our front door and hearing a group of costumed youngsters happily shout out the traditional Halloween greeting: "(Nothing)."

At least that's what traditionally happens at our house. The youngsters just stand there, silent. They have no idea that I have opened the door. They are as blind as bats, because their eyes are not lined up with the eyeholes in their costume masks.

Poorly aligned eyeholes are an ancient Halloween tradition, dating back at least as far as my childhood in Armonk, New York. My early Halloween memories consist of staggering around disguised as a ghost, unable to see anything except the bed sheet and consequently bonking into trees, falling into brooks, etc. The highlight of my ghost career came in the 1954 Halloween parade, when I marched directly into the butt of a horse.

Today's children, of course, do not wear bed sheets. They wear manufactured costumes representing licensed Saturday-morning cartoon characters and purchased from the Toys "Я" A Billion-Dollar Industry store, but I am pleased to note that the eyeholes still don't line up. So when I open the door on Halloween, I am confronted with three or four imaginary heroes such as G.I. Joe, Conan the Barbarian, Oliver North, etc., all of whom would look very terrifying except that they are three feet tall and facing in random directions. They stand there silently for several seconds, then an adult voice hisses from the darkness behind them: "Say 'Trick or Treat,' dammit!"

This voice of course belongs to good old Dad, who wants more than anything to be home watching the World Series and eating taco dip in bulk, but who must instead accompany the children on their trick-or-treat rounds to make sure I don't put razor blades in the candy. This is a traditional Halloween danger that the local perky TV news personalities warn us about every year, using the Frowny Face they put on when they have to tell us about Bad News, such as plane crashes and rainy weekends.

So I understand why good old Dad has to be there, but he makes me nervous. I can feel him watching me suspiciously from somewhere out there, and I think to myself: What if he's armed? There is a reasonable concern, because I live in South Florida, where nuns are armed. So I am very careful about the way I hand out treats.

"Well, boys or perhaps girls!" I say to the licensed characters, in a voice so nonthreatening as to make Mr. Rogers sound like Darth Vader. "How about some nice candy in its original packaging that you can clearly see when I hold it up to the porch light here has not been tampered with?" Alerted by the sound of my voice, the licensed characters start lurching blindly toward me, thrusting out trick-or-treat bags already containing enough chocolate to meet the nation's zit needs well into the next century.

8 Of course there is more to Halloween than massive carbohydrate overdoses. There is also the tradition of bitching about pumpkin prices, a tradition that my wife and I enjoy engaging in each year after paying as much as $20 for a dense inedible fruit so that some pumpkin rancher can put a new Jacuzzi in his Lear jet. This is followed by the tradition of scooping the insides, or technically, the "goop," out of the pumpkin, a chore that always falls to me because both my wife and son refuse to do it, and not without reason, what with the alarming increase in pumpkin-transmitted diseases. (Get the facts! Call the American Pumpkin Council! Don't mention my name!)

9 But I consider the risk of permanent disfigurement to be a small price to pay for the excitement that comes when I finally finish carving Mr. Jack O'Lantern and put him out on the front porch, there to provide hours of pleasure for the trick-or-treating youngsters except that (a) they can't see and (b) Mr. Jack O'Lantern immediately gets his face kicked into mush by older youngsters playing pranks.

10 Pranks—defined as "activities that struck you as truly hilarious when you were a teenager but, now that you are a property owner, make you wish you had a high-voltage fence"— are another ancient Halloween tradition. The first Halloween prank ever, played by a group of Druid teenagers, was Stonehenge ("Hey! You kids get those rocks off my lawn!!"). I can't really complain about the pranks, because as a youth I played several thousand myself. In fact, I figure there must be a God of Prank Justice, who keeps track of everything we do when we're young and then uses Halloween to settle the score ("OK, that's his 14th mailbox. He has 57 to go."). Vastly enjoying this spectacle, I bet, are the ghosts of all my former victims. Assuming they can see through their eyeholes.

A Second Look

1. Barry appeals to readers by mentioning several aspects of Halloween that are familiar to everyone who has celebrated that night. What are some of them?

2. How has Halloween changed since Barry was a boy? How has it remained the same?

3. Writers are often told they should rarely (if ever) begin a sentence with a coordinating conjunction (for example, *and*, *but*, *so*); however, Barry does this frequently. He also ends his essay with a sentence fragment. Why does he deliberately break these "rules" of writing?

4. This essay is loosely organized, but it is not unorganized. Look at the beginnings of paragraphs to see how Barry makes transitions from one point to another.

A Cyberlook

Search under Barry's name on *InfoTrac College Edition* and look for the article by Ron Chepesiuk, which will give you more information about this popular writer. If you like Barry's essays, you can access his columns directly at the *Miami Herald* web site.

Ideas for Writing

Choose an aspect of Halloween (or some other holiday) that you find amusing, and describe it from your personal point of view. If you choose a holiday with which some of your readers may be unfamiliar, briefly explain its significance and a few of its traditions.

This type of essay is fun to write and to read, but remember that informal writing is not disorganized writing. Be sure that your reader can follow your ideas clearly from paragraph to paragraph.

The First Kiss

Steven Graves

Looking Forward

In this freshman essay, a student remembers an important event in his life. Notice that the amused attitude is that of the mature Steven Graves looking back, not that of young Stevie Graves, the first-grader being described.

Help with Words

burr-headed *(paragraph 1):* having a short haircut
incredible *(paragraph 1):* unbelievable
virile *(paragraph 2):* manly
knickers *(paragraph 4):* knee-length pants

Of parades and circus trips and all those anxiously awaited jaunts to Grandmother's or the ice cream parlor, the most memorable occasion of all was my first kiss. The electricity that went through my body and soul was enough to light Manhattan. Every hair on my burr-headed little body stood on end. The nights afterward weren't long enough to handle the incredible dreams that rushed through my head.

There I was, Stevie Graves, "Peaches" to my friends, young and virile, finely tuned body, masculine approach to problems, and sporting one of the most beautiful flattops in the first grade at Ewing Elementary School. My uncle, who was older, a fourth grader, had explained the process of the first kiss to me, and I was ready. He went on to explain more, but I decided I would perfect one thing at a time.

Now I'm not saying I didn't already have a grasp of kissing. My mother and dad never kissed when I could see them, but my cousin Jane was all lips. She and her boyfriend used to kiss for hours and hours, even days. I thought they were going to die from lack of air once. I couldn't see much except lips through that keyhole, but that was enough to cause strange feelings in me.

I had been in love with a girl named Debbie ever since I started kindergarten, and I knew that when the moment was just right, she was going to be the one. And she was. There I stood, grammar book in one hand, a copy of *Daisy the Cow* in the other, and my knickers bound tight around my knees. No, that's a lie. I never had knickers, but my stance on the front steps of the school that day must have looked very noble anyway.

We had been writing to each other for months about getting together for a kiss or two, but now it was going to happen. Here she came off the bus, bouncing like a basketball, hair in braids, teeth in braces, just bursting with youth and excitement, ready for—yes, the kiss. She ran towards me, and I knew it was now. She passed me by, but then she turned, ran back, and planted the most beautiful kiss on my cheek. I was electric, caught at the top of the Ferris wheel of first-grade sexual response.

As years passed, I forgot about Debbie, but that kiss will always be a place, a time, an experience I'll never forget. If only I could be there again, waiting anxiously to be swept off my feet by a gentle peck on the cheek.

A Second Look

1. How does the author create humor in this essay?

2. The essay is not as loosely organized as it first appears to be. Briefly outline the organization.

3. Pick out several descriptive words or phrases, and explain why you consider them to be effective. Pay particular attention to paragraph 5.

Ideas for Writing

1. Tell about an emotion-filled experience from your elementary-school days. This kind of paper needs careful organization. Begin by indicating the subject (such as a first kiss) and setting up the situation. Then tell about the event itself. Be sure the action is described in the order in which it occurred. If you wish, you may close by looking back from the present and commenting on this emotional experience.

2. In a paragraph, describe yourself as a first-grader. Include details about your appearance and your feelings. Your description may be completely factual, or like Steven Graves's self-portrait, it may include slight humorous exaggeration.

Big Mike

Jason Flanary

Looking Forward

Jason Flanary, asked to write an extended definition of a common term, thought of "family fight." His next thought was of his father, Big Mike, who has developed his own ways of dealing with disagreements. Big Mike's tactics may not be fair, but they are successful, as is Flanary's humorous description of them. This student essay was written in class.

Help with Words

squared circle *(paragraph 1):* a boxing ring
arsenal *(paragraph 2):* a collection or weapons and ammunition

Slamming doors, yelling, and the occasional throwing of loose objects often define a family fight. But when you step into the squared circle with Big Mike, family feuding takes on a whole new meaning. Big Mike, more commonly known as Dad, has redefined the meaning of a family squabble for me. When I see family fights on TV sitcoms like *The Cosby Show*, *Family Matters*, or *Full House*, they usually have two sides with two different points of view being voiced. Our family fights, however, turn into a one-sided, one-voiced lecture, more like the comedy genius of *Roseanne*.

Big Mike—standing at a stout 6'2", 315 pounds, and having the deepest voice ever given to man—can strike fear into anyone. His biggest flaw is that he loves to argue. (Oh yes, he is always right, too.) When he steps into the ring, we prepare for war because be brings a whole arsenal with him. He uses various techniques to get his point across. His best weapon is to talk loud without letting anyone else speak and then to retreat. If he needs to dip further into his bag of tricks, he can pull out the yell-so-loud-no-one-understands or the even more underhanded ramble-on-for-hours-until-everyone-gives-up. With these weapons he equips himself for a battle that he always wins.

Let's take an argument over the grocery bill. With my family this bill can become quite excessive, and this doesn't set well with Big Mike. Ding, ding, ding. Fighters, take your corners and come out swinging.

"This bill is too high; you spend too much money," Big Mike yells.

"Well, if you didn't eat all the food, it wouldn't be," Mom replies.

The gloves are off, and Big Mike dips into his bag. He pulls out the ever-reliable talk-loud-and-retreat. Yelling at the top of his lungs, he gets his point across as fast as he can and then rushes into the bedroom and shuts the door. Success. He has made his point, no one else has talked, and once again he was right. Another one-sided lecture given by Big Mike.

Family disagreements have always taken this or a similar form in my household. To me, the definition of family fight has always been a one-sided argument. Big Mike can take control of a situation faster than anyone else in the family. If there is a battle, you can bet Big Mike is right in the middle of it using any means necessary to gain victory. Talk loud and retreat, yell so loud no one understands, or ramble on for hours—a family fight in my home will always come out a one-sided, one-voiced lecture.

A Second Look

1. The writer introduced us to Flanary family fights by referring to several TV shows (paragraph 1)? Why does he do this? Do you think the technique is effective?

2. *Tone* refers to a writer's attitude toward his or her subject. How would you describe Flanary's tone in this essay?

3. There are two major metaphors in this essay, both comparing family fights to other violent activities. What are these metaphors? Find the places where Flanary refers to them.

4. The writer concludes by restating his main point, borrowing language from paragraphs 1 and 2. Do you consider the conclusion effective or too repetitive?

Ideas for Writing

Is there someone in your family or circle of friends who is always dominant, always right, but is still viewed with great affection as well as amusement? Describe this person.

Making Connections

As the introductory note to this unit stated, humor can be used to make a serious point. Which of the essays included in this unit have a serious point? What are the points they make? Why is humor sometimes an effective way to communicate serious ideas?

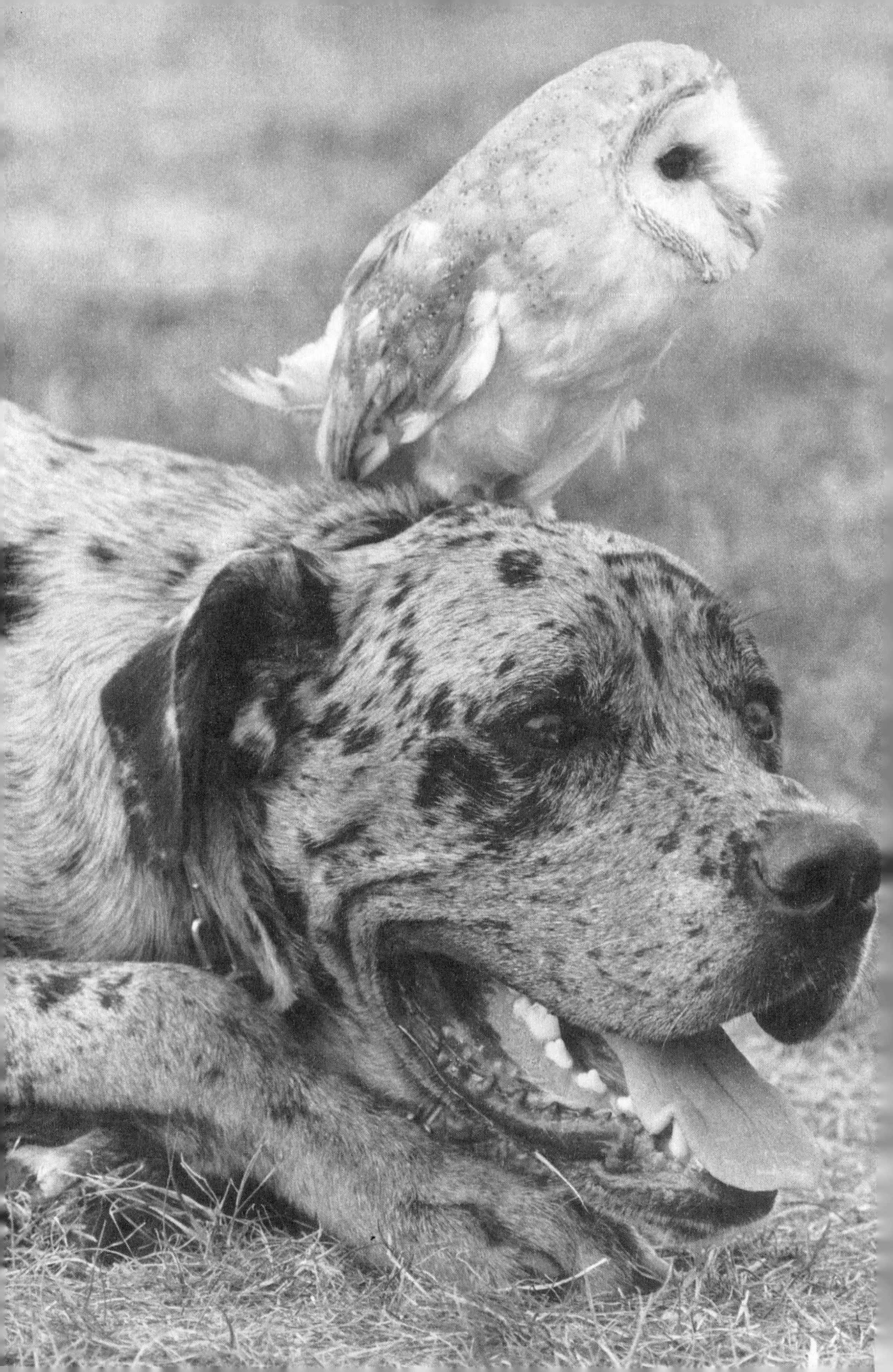

Differences

According to a popular phrase, we "Celebrate Diversity." But do we really? Humanity is characterized by its astonishing differences—cultural, racial, intellectual, physical, spiritual—yet we often seem to believe that others should be just like us. In the essays that follow, four writers reflect on the things that make them distinct and wonder why others sometimes find it difficult to accept these distinctions. None of the writers sought the qualities or conditions that make them different, but they acknowledge them. With dignity, self-respect, even pride, they accept who they are. Surely we can do no less.

Halfway to Dick and Jane

Jack Agueros

Looking Forward

The son of Puerto Rican immigrants, Jack Agueros grew up in Spanish Harlem. The differences he writes about are caused by both passing time and varying ethnic backgrounds. He finds himself caught between two cultures—halfway.

Help with Words

dismantle *(paragraph 2):* take apart
plantain *(paragraph 2):* a large plant with leaves and fruit similar to the banana
compensation *(paragraph 2):* payment
foyer *(paragraph 2):* entrance hall
declaim *(paragraph 2):* recite dramatically
immaculate *(paragraph 3):* spotlessly clean
railroad flat *(paragraph 5):* a narrow apartment with the rooms connecting in a single line and with doors front and back
intensified *(paragraph 7):* made stronger
pathetically *(paragraph 7):* very sadly
pathologically *(paragraph 7):* in an unhealthy or diseased way

I am an only child. My parents and I always talked about my becoming a doctor. The law and politics were not highly regarded in my house. Lawyers, my mother would explain, had to defend people whether they were guilty or not, while politicians, my father would say, were all crooks. A doctor helped everybody, rich and poor, white and black. If I became a doctor, I could study hay fever and find a cure for it, my godmother would say. Also, I could take care of my parents when they were old. I liked the idea of helping, and for nineteen years my sole ambition was to study medicine.

My house had books, not many, but my parents encouraged me to read. As I became a good reader they bought books for me and never refused me money for their purchase. My father once built a bookcase for me. It was an important moment, for I had always believed that my father was not too happy about my being a bookworm. The atmosphere at home was always warm. We seemed to be a popular family. We entertained frequently, with two standing parties a year—at Christmas and for my birthday. Parties were always large. My father would dismantle the beds and move all the furniture so that the full two rooms could be used for dancing. My mother would cook up a storm, particularly at Christmas. *Pasteles, lechon asado, arroz con gandules,* and a lot of *coquito* to drink (meat-stuffed plantain, roast pork, rice with pigeon peas, and coconut nog). My father always brought in a band. They played without compensation and were guests at the party. They ate and drank and danced while a victrola covered the intermissions. One year my father brought home a whole pig and hung it in the foyer doorway. He and my mother prepared it by rubbing it down with oil, oregano, and garlic. After preparation, the pig was taken down and carried over to a local bakery where it was cooked and returned home. Parties always went on till daybreak, and in addition to the band, there were always volunteers to sing and declaim poetry.

My mother kept an immaculate household. Bedspreads (chenille seemed to be very in) and lace curtains, washed at home like everything else, were hung up on huge racks with rows of tight nails. The racks were assembled in the living room, and the moisture from the wet bedspreads would fill the apartment. In a sense, that seems to be the lasting image of that period of my life. The house was clean. The neighbors were clean. The streets, with few cars, were clean. The buildings were clean and uncluttered with people on the stoops. The park was clean. The visitors to my house were clean, and the relationships that my family had with other Puerto Rican families, and the Italian families that my father had met through baseball and my mother through the garment center, were clean. Second Avenue was clean and most of the apartment windows had awnings. There was always music, there seemed to be no rain, and snow did not become slush. School was fun, we wrote essays about how grand America was, we put up hunchbacked cats at Halloween, we believed Santa Claus visited everyone. I believed everyone was Catholic. I grew up with dogs, nightingales, my godmother's guitar, rocking chair, cat, guppies, my father's occasional roosters, kept in a cage on the fire escape. Laundry delivered and collected by horse and wagon, fruits and vegetables sold the same way, windowsill refrigeration in winter, iceman and box in summer. The police my friends, likewise the teachers.

4   In short, the first seven or so years of my life were not too great a variation on Dick and Jane, the school book figures who, if my memory serves me correctly, were blond Anglo-Saxons, not immigrants, not migrants like the Puerto Ricans, and not the children of either immigrants or migrants.

5   My family moved in 1941 to Lexington Avenue into a larger apartment where I could have my own room. It was a light, sunny, railroad flat on the top floor of a well-kept building. I transferred to a new school, and whereas before my classmates had been mostly black, the new school had few blacks. The classes were made up of Italians, Irish, Jews, and a sprinkling of Puerto Ricans. My block was populated by Jews, Italians, and Puerto Ricans.

6   And then a whole series of different events began. I went to junior high school. We played in the backyards, where we tore down fences to build fires to cook stolen potatoes. We tore up whole hedges, because the green tender limbs would not burn when they were peeled, and thus made perfect skewers for our

stolen "mickies." We played tag in the abandoned buildings, tearing the plaster off the walls, tearing the wire lath off the wooden slats, tearing the wooden slats themselves, good for fires, for kites, for sword fighting. We ran up and down the fire escapes playing tag and over and across many rooftops. The war ended and the heavy Puerto Rican migration began. The Irish and the Jews disappeared from the neighborhood. The Italians tried to consolidate east of Third Avenue.

What caused the clean and open world to end? Many things. Into an ancient neighborhood came pouring four to five times more people than it had been designed to hold. Men who came running at the promise of jobs were jobless as the war ended. They were confused. They could not see the economic forces that ruled their lives as they drank beer on the corners, reassuring themselves of good times to come while they were hell-bent toward alcoholism. The sudden surge in numbers caused new resentments, and prejudice was intensified. Some were forced to live in cellars, and were then characterized as cave dwellers. Kids came who were confused by the new surroundings; their Puerto Ricanness forced us against a mirror asking, "If they are Puerto Ricans, what are we?" and thus they confused us. In our confusion we were sometimes pathetically reaching out, sometimes pathologically striking out. Gangs. Drugs. Wine. Smoking. Girls. Dances and slow-drag music. Mambo. Spics, Spooks, and Wops. Territories, brother gangs, and war councils establishing rules for right of way on blocks and avenues and for seating in the local theater. Pegged pants and zip guns. Slang.

Dick and Jane were dead, man. Education collapsed. Every classroom had ten kids who spoke no English. Black, Italian, Puerto Rican relations in the classroom were good, but we all knew we couldn't visit one another's neighborhoods. Sometimes we could not move too freely within our own blocks. On 109th, from the lamp post west, the Latin Aces, and from the lamp post east, the Senecas, the "club" I belonged to. The kids who spoke no English became known as Marine Tigers, picked up from a popular Spanish song. (The Marine Tiger and the Marine Shark were two ships that sailed from San Juan to New York and brought over many, many migrants from the island.)

The neighborhood had its boundaries. Third Avenue and east, Italian. Fifth Avenue and west, black. South, there was a hill on 103rd Street known locally as Cooney's Hill. When you got to the top of the hill, something strange happened: America began, because from the hill south was where the "Americans" lived. Dick and Jane were not dead: they were alive and well in a better neighborhood.

When, as a group of Puerto Rican kids, we decided to go swimming to Jefferson Park Pool, we knew we risked a fight and a beating from the Italians. And when we went to La Milagrosa Church in Harlem, we knew we risked a fight and a beating from the blacks. But when we went over Cooney's Hill, we risked dirty looks, disapproving looks, and questions from the police like, "What are you doing in this neighborhood?" and "Why don't you kids go back where you belong?"

Where we belonged! Man, I had written compositions about America. Didn't I belong on the Central Park tennis courts, even if I didn't know how to play? Couldn't I watch Dick play? Weren't these policemen working for me too? . . .

A Second Look

1. Dick and Jane were the white, middle-class characters in a series of reading textbooks once very popular in lower elementary school. What does Agueros mean by "Halfway to Dick and Jane"? What does he mean when he refers to the characters again in paragraphs 8, 9, and 11?

2. What differences occur after Agueros moves to Lexington Avenue? What are the causes of these differences?

3. In paragraph 7, Agueros says that when new immigrant kids moved into the neighborhood, "their Puerto Ricanness forced us against a mirror asking, 'If they are Puerto Ricans, what are we?'" What does he mean by this?

4. Beginning in paragraph 7, there are some changes in the author's style, especially in his word choice and sentence structure. What are these changes, and why do you think he makes them?

5. If you have read "The Woman Warrior" and "My Family's Language," compare the experiences of Maxine Hong Kingston and Richard Rodriguez with those of Jack Agueros. How were their childhoods similar, and how were they different? Do you think Kingston and Rodriguez, as children, would describe themselves as "halfway to Dick and Jane"? Explain why or why not.

A Cyberlook

In small groups, discuss what you remember about the presentation of culturally diverse groups or the representation of diverse peoples in your own elementary and high school textbooks. Then compare your recollections with the information found in Ava L. McCall, "We Were Cheated! Students' Responses to a Multicultural Social Reconstructionist Teacher Education Course." Search for the *University of Wisconsin System Institute on Race and Ethnicity* web site. Scroll down to Kaleidoscope II and click. Then click on Spring 1997; finally, click on the title, "We Were Cheated!" If you have difficulty finding the site, go to the *Wadsworth Developmental English* web page and click on Textbook Resource Centers.

Ideas for Writing

1. If you are the child of immigrant parents (or perhaps if you know well someone else who is), then you too may understand what it is like to be caught between two cultures. If so, describe this feeling. Explain how it feels to move away from one culture and toward another. You might consider such questions as these: Do you feel good or bad about this experience? Are you moving voluntarily from one culture to another, or do you feel you are being forced? Do you resent either cultural group or perhaps both? What are the advantages and disadvantages of the move? Use specific details and brief descriptions of specific experiences to show your readers how you feel. Assume that your readers are of various ethnic or cultural backgrounds; that is, they are not all Hispanic, all black, all white, and so on.

2. A policeman says to Agueros and his friends: "Why don't you kids go back where you belong?" Has anyone ever made you feel as if you didn't belong? If so, describe that experience. Tell your readers what the situation was, who said you did not belong, and how you reacted to that charge.

3. Have you ever lived in a neighborhood or a community that went through a major change, growing either better or worse? If so, write about the experience. Explain to your readers (who may not be familiar with the place you are describing) how the place was before the change and then after. Also explain the reasons the change occurred. (You may wish to look again at paragraphs 5–9 of "Halfway to Dick and Jane.")

Thoughts While Putting on Mascara Before Giving a Keynote Address

Anne Barrett Swanson

Looking Forward

Anne Barrett Swanson is an academic dean and a biochemist. The thoughts that she shares in this personal essay relate to the difficulties that she experiences because of her "differences": She is three feet seven inches tall and walks with a cane.

Help with Words

contours *(paragraph 1):* the outline of a figure, especially one that curves
function *(paragraph 2):* the activity for which a space is particularly fitted
compatriots *(paragraph 2):* colleagues
access codes *(paragraph 2):* legal requirements guaranteeing the handicapped equal rights to enter and move through public places
juxtaposition *(paragraph 3):* placement of two things side by side, especially for comparison
preconceptions *(paragraph 3):* opinions arrived at before actual knowledge
aberrant *(paragraph 7):* different from the normal

I need a bit more blusher on my cheekbones. Last week at the teacher's convention, it didn't matter as much. But tonight my audience is a group of architects, and architects probably notice contours and construction, even in the face. Will I be successful? Will I be able to shift their awareness, ever so gradually, from the way I look and the construction of my body, my legs and my cane, to the construction of their buildings and their spaces?

Spaces, full of clean lines and light and function, but not for me and my compatriots, not when some of us can't get in the door. The access codes, they will say, are for public places but not for laboratories and workstations. The codes are for hospital rooms so we can be good patients, but those codes need not apply to the medical labs because that's where productive people do important work.

So until there are access codes and laws for those places where we want to learn and work, I must rely on my words and my face. And on my audience's surprise at the juxtaposition of my reality with their preconceptions about disabled people.

Green eyeshadow will add a little drama. I remember what Rob said about times like this: "You're on the chicken salad circuit now. Don't forget to call me and tell me when you know you've batted 1,000 that day." Some days I did, and some days I didn't, but I usually called Rob anyway. Rob was one of the earliest fighters for our cause, and he knew how important that phone call was to remind me of the team out there pulling for me. You died way too soon, Rob. Maybe it was too much chicken salad.

I'd better touch up that mascara on my left eye. I really should get the waterproof kind. Once, at a scientists' meeting, I met a woman in a sensible suit. She raked me over the coals for wearing makeup and a flowing skirt and a long red silk scarf around my neck. She said I was broadcasting that I was a woman, not a scientist, and if I got more secure and embraced the women's movement, I would stop dressing in such a silly way to attract the attention of men.

Such strange bedfellows we are, the women's movement and this cause of ours which is emerging as a disability rights movement. The women of my cause are struggling to be recognized as capable and smart, and powerful, and not helpless, just as the woman in the sensible suit was.

But we are also struggling to be acknowledged as women, to be part of the human family, and sensual and attractive, no matter the construction of our bodies; to be considered okay, not aberrant, if we are wives and moms. The woman in the sensible suit was fighting against being forced to be those very things that we are fighting for the right to become.

Just a little gloss over my lipstick and then I'm done. On the chicken salad circuit, what is more powerful, my words or my face? To speak words of power to these architects tonight, or to twinkle and laugh at my own jokes, flaunt my new dress and put them at ease with this alien who will show them she really is a member of their family after all?

Fifteen minutes are left before the pre-conference reception begins. I'll go downstairs early and make sure the hotel convention manager put in that lowered podium I asked for, and check whether I can easily climb the platform. Maybe I'll bat 1,000 with the architects tonight. If I do, Rob, I'll call you.

A Second Look

1. At what point in the essay is it clear that the author is physically handicapped?

2. Restate in your own words the exact point that Swanson hopes her speech to the architects will make. Why does she apply makeup to reinforce her speech?

3. The writer uses the application of her makeup to give order to her essay. Identify the paragraphs with references to makeup, and describe how these references contribute to the overall organization of the essay.

4. Makeup is also used to clarify the point that Swanson is making about the differences between the women's rights movement and the disability rights movement. What are some of these differences?

A Cyberlook

Swanson mentions that access for the handicapped is limited. Her article was written shortly after the passage of the Americans with Disabilities

Act of 1990. After nearly a decade, that law has opened up a number of areas for the handicapped, but it has also caused a great deal of controversy. For more information on this act and its effects, search *InfoTrac College Edition*. To find out the very latest legislative changes or proposed changes, you can search *THOMAS: Legislative Information on the Internet*, a site maintained by the Library of Congress. If you have difficulty finding the site, go to the *Wadsworth Developmental English* web page and click on Textbook Resource Centers.

Ideas for Writing

Find out what is done on your campus to ensure equal access for physically handicapped students. You might consult the college catalog, student handbook, or other school publications. Learn who is chiefly responsible for ensuring equal access or find who on the staff counsels handicapped students, and interview those people. If you know handicapped students in your classes or your dorm, ask questions of them. When you have collected enough information, write an essay in which you tell what your school has done to guarantee equal access and indicate what further steps need to be taken. If your instructor wishes, you may work in small groups to gather information and even write group reports.

On Being Seventeen, Bright, and Unable to Read

David Raymond

Looking Forward

David Raymond's difference is his inability to read—not because of any lack of training but because of dyslexia. This condition, which prevents a person from recognizing words and sometimes even numbers, results from a brain dysfunction. As Raymond's title suggests, dyslexia is unrelated to intelligence. Notice that Raymond opens with a specific example and then introduces his main idea in paragraph 2.

Help with Words

facilities *(paragraph 14):* places or equipment designed for special purposes

One day a substitute teacher picked me to read aloud from the textbook. When I told her, "No, thank you," she came unhinged. She thought I was acting smart, and told me so. I kept calm, and that got her madder and madder. We must have spent ten minutes trying to solve the problem, and finally she got so red in the face I thought she'd blow up. She told me she'd see me after class.

Maybe someone like me was a new thing for that teacher. But she wasn't new to me. I've been through scenes like that all my life. You see, even though I'm seventeen and a junior in high school, I can't read because I have dyslexia. I'm told I read "at a fourth-grade level," but from where I sit, that's not reading. You can't know what that means unless you've been there. It's not easy to tell how it feels when you can't read your homework assignments or the newspaper or a menu in a restaurant or even notes from your own friends.

My family began to suspect I was having problems almost from the first day I started school. My father says my early years in school were the worst years of his life. They weren't so good for me, either. As I look back on it now, I can't find the words to express how bad it really was. I wanted to die. I'd come home from school screaming, "I'm dumb. I'm dumb—I wish I were dead!"

I guess I couldn't read anything at all then—not even my own name—and they tell me I didn't talk as good as other kids. But what I remember about those days is that I couldn't throw a ball where it was supposed to go, I couldn't learn to swim, and I wouldn't learn to ride a bike, because no matter what anyone told me, I knew I'd fail.

Sometimes my teachers would try to be encouraging. When I couldn't read the words on the board they'd say, "Come on, David, you know that word." Only I didn't. And it was embarrassing. I just felt dumb. And dumb was how the kids treated me. They'd make fun of me every chance they got, asking me to spell "cat" or something like that. Even if I knew how to spell it, I wouldn't; they'd only give me another word. Anyway, it was awful, because more than anything I wanted friends. On my birthday when I blew out the candles I didn't wish I could learn to read; what I wished for was that the kids would like me.

With the bad reports coming from school, and with me moaning about wanting to die and how everybody hated me, my parents began looking for help. That's when the testing started. The school tested me, the child guidance center tested me, private psychiatrists tested me. Everybody knew something was wrong—especially me.

7   It didn't help much when they stuck a fancy name onto it. I couldn't pronounce it then—I was only in second grade—and I was ashamed to talk about it. Now it rolls off my tongue, because I've been living with it for a lot of years—dyslexia.

8   All through elementary school it wasn't easy. I was always having to do things that were "different," things the other kids didn't have to do. I had to go to a child psychiatrist, for instance.

9   One summer my family forced me to go to a camp for children with reading problems. I hated the idea, but the camp turned out pretty good, and I had a good time. I met a lot of kids who couldn't read and somehow that helped. The director of the camp said I had a higher IQ than 90 percent of the population. I didn't believe him.

10   About the worst thing I had to do in fifth and sixth grade was go to a special education class in another school in our town. A bus picked me up, and I didn't like that at all. The bus also picked up emotionally disturbed kids and retarded kids. It was like going to a school for the retarded. I always worried that someone I knew would see me on that bus. It was a relief to go to the regular junior high school.

11   Life began to change for me then, because I began to feel better about myself. I found the teachers cared; they had meetings about me and I worked harder for them for a while. I began to work on the potter's wheel, making vases and pots that the teachers said were pretty good. Also, I got a letter for being on the track team. I could always run pretty fast.

12   At high school the teachers are good and everyone is trying to help me. I've gotten honors some marking periods and I've won a letter on the cross-country team. Next quarter I think the school might hold a show of my pottery. I've got some friends. But there are still some embarrassing times. For instance, every time there is writing in the class, I get up and go to the special education room. Kids ask me where I go all the time. Sometimes I say "To Mars."

13   Homework is a real problem. During free periods in school I go into the special ed room and staff members read assignments to me. When I get home my mother reads to me. Sometimes she reads an assignment into a tape recorder and then I go into my room and listen to it. If we have a novel or something like that to read, she reads it out loud to me. Then I sit down with her and we

do the assignment. She'll write, while I talk my answers to her. Lately, I've taken to dictating into a tape recorder, and then someone—my father, a private tutor, or my mother—types up what I've dictated. Whatever homework I do takes someone else's time, too. That makes me feel bad.

We had a big meeting in school the other day—eight of us, four from the guidance department, my private tutor, my parents, and me. The subject was me. I said I wanted to go to college, and they told me about colleges that have facilities and staff to handle people like me. That's nice to hear.

As for what happens after college, I don't know and I'm worried about that. How can I make a living if I can't read? Who will hire me? How will I fill out the application form?

The only thing that gives me any courage is the fact that I've learned about well-known people who couldn't read or had other problems and still made it. Like Albert Einstein, who didn't talk until he was four and flunked math. Like Leonardo da Vinci, who everyone seems to think had dyslexia.

I've told this story because maybe some teacher will read it and go easy on a kid in the classroom who has what I've got. Or maybe some parent will stop nagging his kid, and stop calling him lazy. Maybe he's not lazy or dumb. Maybe he just can't read and doesn't know what's wrong. Maybe he's scared, like I was.

A Second Look

1. Besides the inability to read, what were some other early signs of David Raymond's dyslexia?

2. Mention several changes that helped Raymond feel better about himself.

3. Raymond often uses casual words or even slang—for example, "thought she'd blow up" (paragraph 1). Find other examples of this type of language. What impression does this language create?

4. Raymond uses many details from his personal experience. How does he put them in order?

5. In general, this essay explains what has happened to the writer and how he feels about it. The last paragraph, however, serves a different purpose. What is it?

A Cyberlook

Researchers estimate that approximately fifteen percent of the population is dyslexic, yet many cases go undiagnosed, especially in American schools. For more information on this condition, search *InfoTrac College Edition*. If you would like to know more about diagnosis, treatment, support groups, and so forth, access the International Dyslexia Association web site. You may work in groups, if your instructor wishes.

Ideas for Writing

1. Think of a time when you felt different from those around you. What was the difference? Did you look different or talk differently? Could everyone else do something that you could not? As exactly as you can, remember the situation, and recall how you reacted. Were you embarrassed, angry, hurt, or all these? Now write an essay in which you first describe the time when you felt different; then explain why you felt as you did. Finally, tell how you reacted. You will be writing, as David Raymond did, for a group of readers who do not know you.

2. One way of defining something is to explain how it works. David Raymond helps explain what dyslexia is by showing how it affected his life. If you know of some condition like dyslexia that has made a difference in your life or the life of someone you know, help define or explain that condition by showing its effects. You may begin, as Raymond did, with an example, or you may begin by mentioning the condition. Your readers may be familiar with the condition you are explaining, but they do not know you or the person you are writing about.

For My Indian Daughter

Lewis P. Johnson

Looking Forward

Lewis P. Johnson, an Ottawa Indian, recalls an unpleasant experience when he and his family, enjoying a day at the beach, encountered bigotry in an unusually stupid form. The insult to Johnson's family causes him to look back over his long, slow journey toward understanding his own heritage and to wonder how he can make that journey less difficult for his young daughter.

Help with Words

unbidden *(paragraph 1):* unasked for
guttural *(paragraph 2):* low and throaty
affluent *(paragraph 5):* wealthy
comeuppance *(paragraph 7):* a deserved punishment (here used ironically)
discomfiting *(paragraph 13):* causing discomfort, disturbing

My little girl is singing herself to sleep upstairs, her voice mingling with the sounds of the birds outside in the old maple trees. She is two and I am nearly fifty, and I am very taken with her. She came along late in my life, unexpected and unbidden, a startling gift.

Today at the beach my chubby-legged, brown-skinned daughter ran laughing into the water as fast as she could. My wife and I laughed watching her, until we heard behind us a low guttural curse and then an unpleasant voice raised in an imitation war whoop.

I turned to see a fat man in a bathing suit, white and soft as a grub, as he covered his mouth and prepared to make the Indian war cry again. He was middle-aged, younger than I, and had three little children lined up next to him, grinning foolishly. My wife suggested we leave the beach, and I agreed.

I knew the man was not unusual in his feelings against Indians. His beach behavior might have been socially unacceptable to more civilized whites, but his basic view of Indians is expressed daily in our small town, frequently on the editorial pages of the county newspaper, as white people speak out against Indian fishing rights and land rights, saying in essence, "Those Indians are taking our fish, our land." It doesn't matter to them that we were here first, that the U.S. Supreme Court has ruled in our favor. It matters to them that we have something they want, and they hate us for it. Backlash is the common explanation of the attacks on Indians, the bumper stickers that say, "Spear an Indian, Save a Fish," but I know better. The hatred of Indians goes back to the beginning when white people came to this country. For me it goes back to my childhood in Harbor Springs, Mich.

Theft: Harbor Springs is now a summer resort for the very affluent, but a hundred years ago it was the Indian village of my Ottawa ancestors. My grandmother, Anna Showanessy, and other Indians like her, had their land there taken by treaty, by fraud, by violence, by theft. They remembered how whites had burned down the village at Burt Lake in 1900 and pushed the Indians out. These were the stories in my family.

When I was a boy my mother told me to walk down the alleys in Harbor Springs and not to wear my orange football sweater out of the house. This way I could not stand out, not be noticed, and not be a target.

I wore my orange sweater anyway and deliberately avoided the alleys. I was the biggest person I knew and wasn't really afraid. But I met my comeuppance when I enlisted in the U.S. Army. One night all the men in my barracks gathered together and, gang-fashion, pulled me into the shower and scrubbed me down with rough brushes used for floors, saying, "We won't have any dirty Indians in our outfit." It is a point of irony that I was cleaner than any of them. Later in Korea I learned how to kill, how to bully, how to hate Koreans. I came out of the war tougher than ever and, strangely, white.

I went to college, got married, lived in La Porte, Indiana, worked as a surveyor and raised three boys. I headed Boy Scout groups, never thinking it odd when the Scouts did imitation Indian dances, imitation Indian lore.

One day when I was thirty-five or thereabouts I heard about an Indian powwow. My father used to attend them and so with great curiosity and a strange joy at discovering a part of my heritage, I decided the thing to do to get ready for this big event was to have my friend make me a spear in his forge. The steel was fine and blue and iridescent. The feathers on the shaft were bright and proud.

In a dusty state fairground in southern Indiana, I found white people dressed as Indians. I learned they were "hobbyists," that is, it was their hobby and leisure pastime to masquerade as Indians on weekends. I felt ridiculous with my spear, and I left.

It was years before I could tell anyone of the embarrassment of this weekend and see any humor in it. But in a way it was that weekend, for all its silliness, that was my awakening. I realized I didn't know who I was. I didn't have an Indian name. I didn't speak the Indian language. I didn't know the Indian customs. Dimly I remembered the Ottawa word for dog, but it was a baby word, *kahgee*, not the full word, *muhkahgee*, which I was later to learn. Even more hazily I remembered a naming ceremony (my own). I remembered legs dancing around me, dust. Where had that been? Who had I been? "*Suwaukquat*," my mother told me when I asked, "where the tree begins to grow."

That was 1968, and I was not the only Indian in the country who was feeling the need to remember who he or she was. There were others. They had powwows, real ones, and eventually I found them. Together we researched our past, a search that for me culminated in the Longest Walk, a march on Washington in 1978.

Maybe because I now know what it means to be Indian, it surprises me that others don't. Of course there aren't very many of us left. The chances of an average person knowing an average Indian in an average lifetime are pretty slim.

Circle: Still, I was amused one day when my small, four-year-old neighbor looked at me as I was hoeing in my garden and said, "You aren't a real Indian, are you?" Scotty is little, talkative, likable. Finally I said, "I'm a real Indian." He looked at me for a moment and then said, squinting into the sun, "Then where's your horse and feathers?" The child was simply a smaller, whiter version of my own ignorant self years before. We'd both seen too much TV, that's all. He was not to be blamed. And so, in a way, the moronic man on the beach today is blameless. We come full circle to realize other people are like ourselves, as discomfiting as that may be sometimes.

As I sit in my old chair on my porch, in a light that is fading so the leaves are barely distinguishable against the sky, I can picture my girl asleep upstairs. I would like to prepare her for what's to come, take her each step of the way saying, there's a place to avoid, here's what I know about this, but much of what's before her she must go through alone. She must pass through pain and joy and solitude and community to discover her own inner self that is unlike any other and come through that passage to the place where she sees all people are one, and in so seeing may live her life in a brighter future.

A Second Look

1. According to Johnson, the prejudice against American Indians is not the result of simple backlash against their recent activism. What are the deeper causes of this prejudice?

2. Johnson says that after the Korean War he left the army "tougher than ever and, strangely, white" (paragraph 7). What does he mean by this statement?

3. The writer uses two subheadings: Theft and Circle. What is stolen? How are his experiences circular?

4. In the opening and closing paragraphs, Johnson "frames" his essay with pictures of himself, sitting alone and thinking of his daughter. Is this device effective, or would Johnson make his point more forcefully if he opened with paragraph 2 and closed with paragraph 13?

A Cyberlook

1. Johnson writes: "Maybe because I now know what it means to be an Indian, it surprises me that others don't. Of course there aren't many of us left" (paragraph 12). What does it mean *statistically* to be an American Indian? For figures on population, income, education, and so forth, see Karen N. Peart, "First Americans" on *InfoTrac College Edition.* Johnson also mentions Indian land and fishing rights, issues that may have a huge economic and social impact on a number of states. To learn more about these topics, see the subdivisions under "Native Americans" on *InfoTrac.*

2. A great deal of information by, about, or of interest to Native Americans is available at *Code Talk*, a government site maintained by Native Americans. In small groups, search some of the links at this site to see the variety of material available. If you have difficulty finding the site, go to the *Wadsworth Developmental English* web page and click on Textbook Resource Centers.

3. If you went through elementary and high school learning little about American Indians beyond the usual Thanksgiving or Wild West lore, see what is now available for K-12 students. Visit *Yahooligans: Native Americans.* Perhaps your class may discuss these topics: How does the Internet influence young minds? How can Internet information serve to develop either tolerance or hatred?

Ideas for Writing

1. Americans are often fast moving and far moving, and many lose touch with their own heritage. We must grow and change, of course, but we often find we have loosened the connections to the generations that came before us. Write an essay in which you examine this issue in your own life. Are you in touch with your own heritage, or have these ties become loosened or broken?

2. Write a letter to a real or imagined ancestor of at least three generations ago (a great-grandparent or earlier). Explain to him or her what part of your heritage you have kept and what part you feel you have lost. Are there parts that you want to recover? Are there other parts that you want or need to leave behind?

Making Connections

Jack Agueros, Anne Barrett Swanson, David Raymond, and Lewis P. Johnson write about differences that can lead to different types of discrimination. What are the types? Are some more damaging than others? What are some of the ways to eliminate such discriminatory behavior?

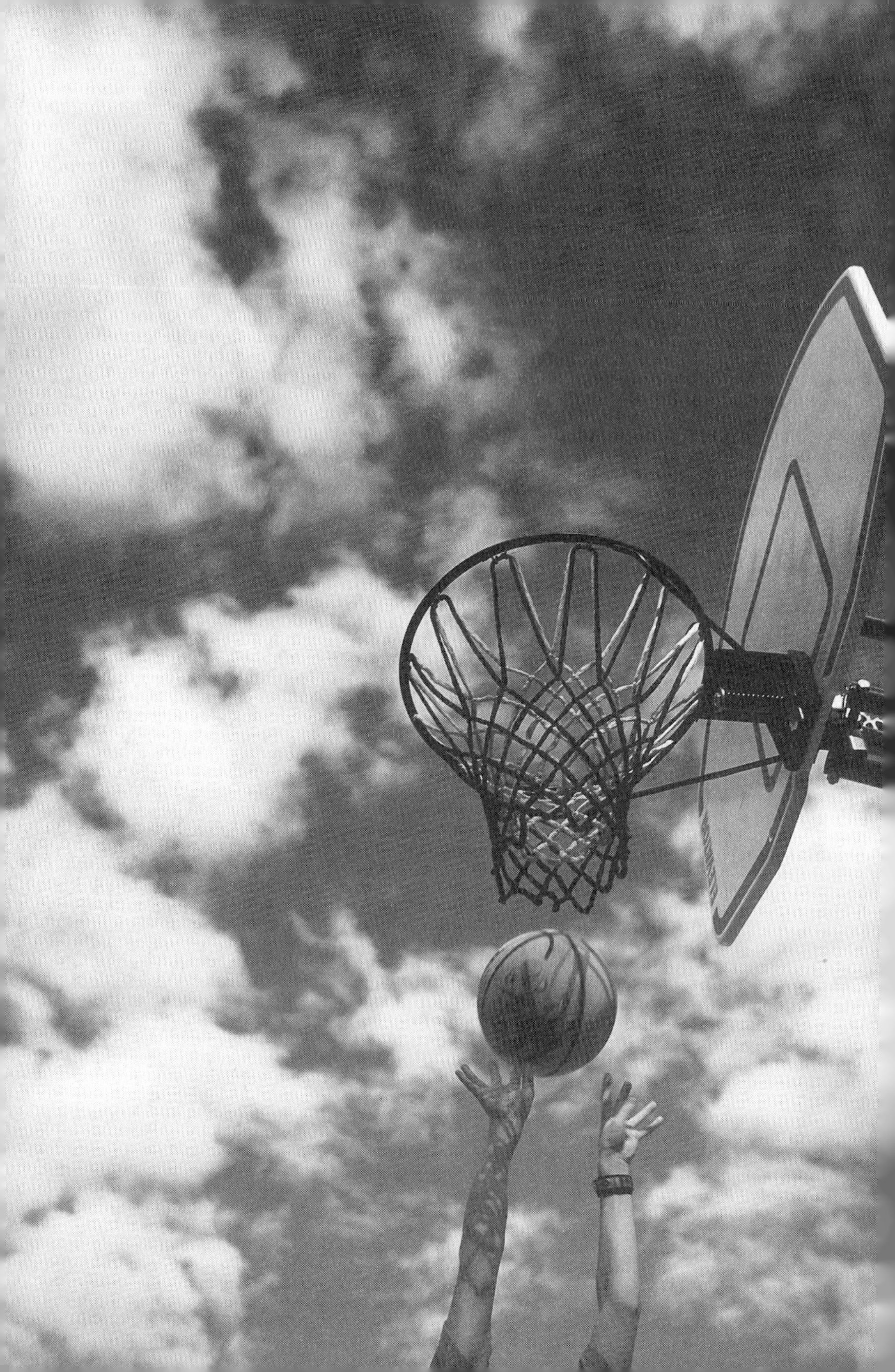

Sports

Sports surround us. Men's, women's, professional, amateur, collegiate, school, youth league—sports are woven into the lives of many people the world over. The writers in this unit approach the topic from various points of view. Stephen King describes the excitement of competition and the agony of losing. Arthur Ashe and John Updike remind us that sports can have a negative as well as a positive influence. A *Time* writer and student Jacquelyn Gist look at the advances in women's athletics. And Evan Carnes suggests that we pay more attention to smart, not dumb, jocks.

Head Down

Stephen King

Looking Forward

In this excerpt from a longer article, Stephen King takes a close look at a few very important moments for a group of preteen boys: the closing minutes of a Little League championship game. Bangor West is playing Hampden for the Penobscot County (Maine) title. It is now the bottom of the last inning. Hampden leads 14 to 12; Bangor West is at bat.

Help with Words

Hampden Horns *(paragraph 2):* Hampden fans who blow automobile and truck horns to cheer their players and intimidate the opposition

silhouettes *(paragraph 8):* outlines

Last call for Bangor West. Jeff Carson, whose fourth-inning home run is really the difference in this game, and who earlier replaced Mike Wentworth on the mound for Hampden, is now replaced by Mike Tardif. He faces Owen King first. King goes three and two (swinging wildly for the fences at one pitch in the dirt), then lays off a pitch just inside to work a walk. Roger Fisher follows him to the plate, pinch-hitting for . . . Fred Moore. Roger is a small boy, with Indian-dark eyes and hair. He looks like an easy out, but looks can be deceptive; Roger has good power. Today, however, he is overmatched. He strikes out.

In the field, the Hampden players shift around and look at each other. They are close, and they know it. The parking lot is too

113

far away here for the Hampden Horns to be a factor; their fans settle for simply screaming encouragement. Two women wearing purple Hampden caps are standing behind the dugout, hugging each other joyfully. Several other fans look like track runners waiting for the starter's gun; it is clear they mean to rush onto the field the moment their boys succeed in putting Bangor West away for good.

Joe Wilcox, who didn't want to be a catcher and ended up doing the job anyway, rams a one-out single up the middle and into left center field. King stops at second. Up steps Arthur Dorr, the Bangor right fielder, who wears the world's oldest pair of high-top sneakers and has not had a hit all day. This time, he hits a shot, but right at the Hampden shortstop, who barely has to move. The shortstop whips the ball to second, hoping to catch King off the bag, but he's out of luck. Nevertheless, there are two out.

The Hampden fans scream further encouragement. The women behind the dugout are jumping up and down. Now there are a few Hampden Horns tootling away someplace, but they are a little early, and all one has to do to know it is to look at Mike Tardif's face as he wipes off his forehead and pounds the baseball into his glove.

Ryan Iarrobino steps into the right-hand batter's box. He has a fast, almost naturally perfect swing. . . .

Ryan swings through Tardif's first pitch, his hardest of the day—it makes a rifle-shot sound as it hits Kyle King's glove. Tardif then wastes one outside. King returns the ball, Tardif meditates briefly, and then throws a low fastball. Ryan looks at it, and the umpire calls strike two. It has caught the outside corner— maybe. The ump says it did, anyway, and that's the end of it.

Now the fans on both sides have fallen quiet, and so have the coaches. They're all out of it. It's only Tardif and Iarrobino now, balanced on the last strike of the last out of the last game one of these teams will play. Forty-six feet between these two faces. Only, Iarrobino is not watching Tardif's face. He is watching Tardif's glove. . . .

Iarrobino is waiting to see how Tardif will come. As Tardif moves to the set position, you can faintly hear the pock-pock, pock-pock of tennis balls on a nearby court, but here there is only silence and the crisp black shadows of the players, lying on the dirt like silhouettes cut from black construction paper, and Iarrobino is waiting to see how Tardif will come.

He comes over the top. And suddenly Iarrobino is in motion, both knees and the left shoulder dipping slightly, the aluminum bat a blur in the sunlight. That aluminum-on-cowhide sound—chink, like someone hitting a tin cup with a spoon—is different this time. A lot different. Not chink but crunch as Ryan connects, and then the ball is in the sky, tracking out to left field—a long shot that is clearly gone, high, wide, and handsome into the summer afternoon. The ball will later be recovered from beneath a car about two hundred and seventy-five feet away from home plate.

The expression on twelve-year-old Mike Tardif's face is stunned, thunderstruck disbelief. He takes one quick look into his glove, as if hoping to find the ball still there and discover that Iarrobino's dramatic two-strike, two-out shot was only a hideous momentary dream. The two women behind the backstop look at each other in total amazement. At first, no one makes a sound. In that moment before everyone begins to scream and the Bangor West players rush out of their dugout to await Ryan at home plate and mob him when he arrives, only two people are entirely sure that it did really happen. One is Ryan himself. As he rounds first, he raises both hands to his shoulders in a brief but emphatic gesture of triumph. And, as Owen King crosses the plate with the first of the three runs that will end Hampden's All-Star season, Mike Tardif realizes. Standing on the pitcher's rubber for the last time as a Little Leaguer, he bursts into tears.

A Second Look

1. King's description causes the reader to take a genuine interest in these young players. How does he make them real people and not merely names?

2. What details help us sense the tension felt by both players and spectators in these closing minutes?

3. What change does King make in his description in paragraphs 7–9? Do you think the change is effective?

4. Why do you think King closes by focusing on the losing pitcher, not the winning runners?

A Cyberlook

You may be surprised to learn that there are many issues—some of them quite controversial—involved in children's sports. If you subscribe to *InfoTrac College Edition,* search the term "sports for children" and its subdivision. You can also access information using your web browser. Working in small groups, compare the results of your search. What are some of the current issues in kids' sports?

Ideas for Writing

1. Describe the winning or losing minutes of a competition in which you participated. (This may be a sports event, but it does not have to be. It could be a speech contest, an academic or musical competition, and so forth.) As King did, use specific details to make the readers feel as if they are there with you. List every detail you can think of related to this experience; as you write, select those that seem most important or fit best into your description.

2. Many people believe that through athletic competition children learn lessons about success and failure that will help them later in life. Tell about an experience in which you or someone you know learned such a lesson.

Send Your Children to the Libraries

Arthur Ashe

Looking Forward

Arthur Ashe played professional tennis for a number of years, winning many awards. He was outstanding in both Wimbledon and Davis Cup competition. But in this letter published in the *New York Times* in 1977, Ashe argues that there are actually few opportunities in professional sports for black athletes. He suggests that there are many roles in society, besides those in sports, that blacks can and should fill. Though the essay was written a number of years ago, it remains popular because Ashe's advice on sports and education is still relevant for many young athletes.

Help with Words

pretentious *(paragraph 2):* falsely superior
expends *(paragraph 3):* spends
dubious *(paragraph 3):* questionable
emulate *(paragraph 4):* follow or imitate
massive *(paragraph 6):* very large
viable *(paragraph 9):* workable
channel *(paragraph 12):* direct

1   Since my sophomore year at University of California, Los Angeles, I have become convinced that we blacks spend too much time on the playing fields and too little time in the libraries.

Please don't think of this attitude as being pretentious just because I am a black, single, professional athlete.

I don't have children, but I can make observations. I strongly believe the black culture expends too much time, energy and effort raising, praising and teasing our black children as to the dubious glories of professional sports.

All children need models to emulate—parents, relatives or friends. But when the child starts school, the influence of the parent is shared by teachers and classmates, by the lure of books, movies, ministers and newspapers, but most of all by television.

Which televised events have the greatest number of viewers? Sports—the Olympics, Super Bowl, Masters, World Series, pro basketball playoffs, Forest Hills. ABC-TV even has sports on Monday night prime time from April to December.

So your child gets a massive dose of O. J. Simpson, Kareem Abdul-Jabbar, Muhammad Ali, Reggie Jackson, Dr. J. and Lee Elder and other pro athletes. And it is only natural that your child will dream of being a pro athlete himself.

But consider these facts: For the major professional sports of hockey, football, basketball, baseball, golf, tennis and boxing, there are roughly only 3,170 major league positions available (attributing 200 positions to golf, 200 to tennis and 100 to boxing). And the annual turnover is small.

We blacks are a subculture of about 28 million. Of the 13½ million men, 5–6 million are under twenty years of age, so your son has less than one chance in a thousand of becoming a pro. Less than one in a thousand. Would you bet your son's future on something with odds of 999 to 1 against you? I wouldn't.

Unless a child is exceptionally gifted, you should know by the time he enters high school whether he has a future as an athlete. But what is more important is what happens if he doesn't graduate or doesn't land a college scholarship and doesn't have a viable alternative job career. Our high school dropout rate is several times the national average, which contributes to our unemployment rate of roughly twice the national average.

And how do you fight the figures in the newspapers every day? Ali has earned more than $30 million boxing, O. J. just signed for $2½ million, Dr. J. for almost $3 million, Reggie Jackson for $2.8 million, Nate Archibald for $400,000 a year. All that money, recognition, attention, free cars, girls, jobs in the off-season—no wonder there is Pop Warner football, Little League baseball, National Junior League tennis, hockey practice at 5 a.m. and pickup basketball games in any center city at any hour.

There must be some way to assure that the 999 who try but don't make it to pro sports don't wind up on the street corners or in the unemployment lines. Unfortunately, our most widely recognized role models are athletes and entertainers—"runnin'" and "jumpin'" and "singin'" and "dancin'." While we are 60 percent of the National Basketball Association, we are less than 4 percent of the doctors and lawyers. While we are about 35 percent of major league baseball, we are less than 2 percent of the engineers. While we are about 40 percent of the National Football League, we are less than 11 percent of construction workers such as carpenters and bricklayers.

Our greatest heroes of the century have been athletes—Jack Johnson, Joe Louis and Muhammad Ali. Racial and economic discrimination forced us to channel our energies into athletics and entertainment. These were the ways out of the ghetto, the ways to that Cadillac, those alligator shoes, that cashmere sport coat.

Somehow, parents must instill a desire for learning alongside the desire to be Walt Frazier. Why not start by sending black professional athletes to high schools to explain the facts of life.

I have often addressed high school audiences and my message is always the same. For every hour you spend on the athletic field, spend two in the library. Even if you make it as a pro athlete, your career will be over by the time you are thirty-five. So you will need that diploma.

Have these pro athletes explain what happens if you break a leg, get a sore arm, have one bad year or don't make the cut for five or six tournaments. Explain to them the star system, wherein for every O. J. earning millions there are six or seven others making $15,000 or $20,000 or $30,000 a year.

But don't just have Walt Frazier or O. J. or Abdul-Jabbar address your class. Invite a benchwarmer or a guy who didn't make it. Ask him if he sleeps every night. Ask him whether he was graduated. Ask him what he would do if he became disabled tomorrow. Ask him where his old high school athletic buddies are.

We have been on the same roads—sports and entertainment—too long. We need to pull over, fill up at the library and speed away to Congress and the Supreme Court, the unions and the business world. We need more Barbara Jordans, Andrew Youngs, union cardholders, Nikki Giovannis and Earl Graveses. Don't worry: We will still be able to sing and dance and run and jump better than anybody else.

I'll never forget how proud my grandmother was when I graduated from UCLA in 1966. Never mind the Davis Cup in 1968, 1969, and 1970. Never mind the Wimbledon title, Forest Hills, etc. To this day, she still doesn't know what those names mean.

What mattered to her was that of her more than thirty children and grandchildren, I was the first to be graduated from college, and a famous college at that. Somehow, that made up for all those floors she scrubbed all those years.

AFTERWORD

After Arthur Ashe first achieved world fame by winning the U.S. Open in 1968, he spoke and wrote often about the importance—in fact, the necessity—of getting a good education. In early April, 1992, Ashe announced that he had tested positive for the AIDS virus. His doctors believed he was infected by a blood transfusion following heart surgery in 1983, two years before blood screening for HIV was required. Ashe revealed his condition reluctantly, not only because he valued his privacy but also because he feared that this news might overshadow the point he has emphasized for over twenty years.

An editorial writer for *The Miami Herald* summarized and commented on the importance of Ashe's message this way:

. . . The odds of a young athlete's becoming a big money star in pro sports are about as good as his chances of winning the lottery.

It is essential, then, that he pursue an education with the same zeal as he pursues success in sports. That, essentially, is Ashe's message. He has worked tirelessly to deliver it to America's young people—especially to those minorities who often see athletics as the only available means of escaping poverty.

Sometimes he's upstaged by the clatter and hype of big-money sports, but that doesn't make his message or his mission any less valid.

Ashe died in 1995.

A Second Look

1. In this letter, Ashe uses many statistics. Are they convincing? Why or why not?
2. What evidence besides statistics does he use to support his main idea?
3. Ashe says, in paragraph 17, "We have been on the same roads—sports and entertainment—too long." Does he mean that blacks should avoid these careers?
4. Ashe's audience consists of parents of black sons. Could his argument apply to other races or to parents of girls? Why or why not?
5. The best piece of evidence to strengthen Ashe's argument may be Ashe himself. How does the letter show this?

A Cyberlook

1. Years after Arthur Ashe's death, his accomplishments and his efforts to improve education for minorities are remembered and admired. For more information, search the Internet using "Arthur Ashe" both as author and subject. If you have access to *InfoTrac College Edition*, search under his name for an article in *Black Collegian* (1995) that named Ashe one of the "Trailblazers . . . for the next generation."
2. Ashe's name has been given to buildings, events, even a university health center. Working in groups, search the Internet and make a list of several of these "memorials" to Ashe. In 1995, ground was broken for a literal memorial, a statue honoring Ashe, in his hometown of Richmond, VA. The statue (or its location, at least) has proved controversial. To learn about this curious case, search "Arthur Ashe memorial" on the Internet.

Ideas for Writing

Write a letter to the editor in which you state an opinion that you feel strongly about. Begin by stating the opinion clearly in a single sentence. Decide who your readers will be. Are you writing for a campus newspaper? A community newspaper? A big-city daily?

    Next, write down all the reasons you can think of why your readers should accept your opinion. Decide which are most effective, and then begin to organize your letter. Begin with your statement of opinion. Follow with support. Near the end, restate the opinion, though not in the same words you used at the beginning.

Ex-Basketball Player

John Updike

Looking Forward

Poet, novelist, and short story writer John Updike has often written about former athletes, like Flick Webb in this poem. In the poem, Updike shows how Flick's life has changed by describing him at work and after work. Pay special attention to Flick's feelings about his past.

Help with Words

tiers *(paragraph 29):* rows rising one behind the other, as in bleachers
Necco Wafers, Nibs, and Juju Beads *(paragraph 30):* brands of candy and snacks

Pearl Avenue runs past the high school lot, 1
   Bends with the trolley tracks, and stops, cut off 2
Before it has a chance to go two blocks, 3
At Colonel McComsky Plaza. Berth's Garage 4
Is on the corner facing west, and there, 5
Most days, you'll find Flick Webb, who helps Berth out. 6

Flick stands tall among the idiot pumps— 7
Five on a side, the old bubble-head style, 8
Their rubber elbows hanging loose and low. 9

122

One's nostrils are two S's, and his eyes
An E and O. And one is squat, without
A head at all—more of a football type.

Once, Flick played for the high school team, the Wizards.
He was good: in fact, the best. In '46,
He bucketed three hundred ninety points,
A county record still. The ball loved Flick.
I saw him rack up thirty-eight or forty
In one home game. His hands were like wild birds.

He never learned a trade; he just sells gas,
Checks oil, and changes flats. Once in a while,
As a gag, he dribbles an inner tube,
But most of us remember anyway.
His hands are fine and nervous on the lug wrench.
It makes no difference to the lug wrench, though.

Off work, he hangs around Mae's Luncheonette.
Grease-grey and kind of coiled, he plays pinball,
Sips lemon cokes, and smokes those thin cigars;
Flick seldom speaks to Mae, just sits and nods
Beyond her face toward the bright applauding tiers
Of Necco Wafers, Nibs, and Juju Beads.

A Second Look

1. Updike shows much about Flick's life by setting up comparisons. How does the description of Pearl Avenue apply to Flick? What is suggested by the description of the pumps?
2. What lines of the poem reveal Flick's talent?
3. What lines show that he lives mainly in the past?

Ideas for Writing

1. Without using Updike's exact words, describe Flick Webb in a paragraph.

2. Have you known someone like Flick Webb, someone who lives on past glory achieved in any field? Describe this person. Tell your readers (who do not know your subject) what kind of success this person had and what kind of person he or she is now.

Comes the Revolution

Time

Looking Forward

The "revolution" in the title refers to the increase in the number of women in sports. The specific examples at the beginning indicate the many types of sports in which women now participate. But, as the article also points out, this is part of a larger change. More and more people are now enjoying sports, regardless of talent, age, or sex. This essay was written over twenty years ago. As you read, consider what has changed and what has not since the essay first appeared.

Help with Words

intensity *(paragraph 1):* strong feeling
charges *(paragraph 1):* those for whom one is responsible
incubator *(paragraph 2):* a machine to aid in the growth of infants or young animals
fanatical *(paragraph 2):* extremely enthusiastic
defiant *(paragraph 2):* rebellious
kaleidoscope *(paragraph 3):* a tube that shows changing patterns of many colors and shapes
buttressed *(paragraph 6):* supported
mandates *(paragraph 6):* orders
stigma *(paragraph 6):* a sign of disgrace
vigor *(paragraph 7):* strength, energy
tenacity *(paragraph 7):* staying power
unseemly *(paragraph 11):* improper
misnomer *(paragraph 11):* wrong name

Steve Sweeney paces the sideline, shoulders hunched against the elements. A steady downpour has turned an Atlanta soccer field into a grassy bog. A few yards away, his team of eight- and nine-year-olds, sporting regulation shirts and shorts, churns after the skittering ball. One minute, all is professional intensity as the players struggle to start a play. The next, there is childhood glee in splashing through a huge puddle that has formed in front of one goal. Sweeney squints at his charges and shouts, "Girls, you gotta pass! Come on, Heather!"

At eight, Kim Edwards is in the incubator of the national pastime—tee-ball. There are no pitchers in the pre-Little League league. The ball is placed on a waist-high, adjustable tee, and for five innings the kids whack away. Kim is one of the hottest tee-ball players in Dayton and a fanatical follower of the Cincinnati Reds. Her position is second base. She pulls a Reds cap down over her hair, punches her glove, drops her red-jacketed arms down to rest on red pants, and waits for the action. Kim has but a single ambition: to play for her beloved Reds. When a male onlooker points out that no woman has every played big league baseball, Kim's face, a mass of strawberry freckles, is a study in defiant dismissal: "So?"

The raw wind of a late-spring chill bites through Philadelphia's Franklin Field, but it cannot dull the excitement of the moment. For the first time in the eighty-four year history of the Penn Relays, the world's largest and oldest meet of its kind, an afternoon of women's track and field competition is scheduled. The infield shimmers with color, a kaleidoscope of uniforms and warmup suits. One thousand college and high school athletes jog slowly back and forth, stretch and massage tight muscles, crouch in imaginary starting blocks, huddle with coaches for last-minute strategy sessions, or loll on the synthetic green turf, sipping cocoa and waiting. Susan White, a nineteen-year-old hurdler from the University of Maryland, surveys the scene. There is a trace of awe in her voice: "When I was in high school, I never dreamed of competing in a national meet. People are finally accepting us as athletes."

Golfer Carol Mann is chatting with friends outside the clubhouse when a twelve-year-old girl walks up, politely clears her throat and asks for an autograph. Mann bends down—it's a long way from six-foot, three-inch Mann to fan—and talks softly as she writes. After several moments, the girl returns, wide-eyed, to waiting parents. Mann straightens and smiles. "Five years ago, little girls never walked up to tell me they wanted to be a professional golfer. Now it happens all the time. Things are changing, things are changing."

They are indeed. On athletic fields and playgrounds and in parks and gymnasiums across the country, a new player has joined the grand game that is sporting competition, and she's a girl. As the long summer begins, not only is she learning to hit a two-fisted backhand like Chris Evert's and turn a back flip like Olga Korbut's, she is also learning to jam a hitter with a fast ball. Season by season, whether aged six, sixty, or beyond, she is running, jumping, hitting and throwing as U.S. women have never done before. She is trying everything from jogging to ice hockey, lacrosse and rugby, and in the process acquiring a new sense of self, and of self-confidence in her physical abilities and her potential. She is leading a revolution that is one of the most exciting and one of the most important in the history of sport. Says Joan Warrington, executive secretary of the Association for Intercollegiate Athletics for Women: "Women no longer feel that taking part in athletics is a privilege. They believe it is a right."

Spurred by the fitness craze, fired up by the feminist movement and buttressed by court rulings and legislative mandates, women have been moving from miniskirted cheerleading on the sidelines for the boys to playing, and playing hard, for themselves. Says Liz Murphy, coordinator of women's athletics at the University of Georgia: "The stigma is nearly erased. Sweating girls are becoming socially acceptable." . . .

If, as folklore and public have long insisted, sport is good for people, if it builds a better society by encouraging mental and physical vigor, courage and tenacity, then the revolution in women's sports holds a bright promise for the future. One city in which the future is now is Cedar Rapids, Iowa. In 1969, well before law, much less custom, required the city to make any reforms, Cedar Rapids opened its public school athletic program to girls and, equally important, to the less gifted boys traditionally squeezed out by win-oriented athletic systems. Says Tom Ecker, head of school athletics, "Our program exists to develop good kids, not to serve as a training ground for the universities and pros."

Some seven thousand students, nearly three thousand of them girls, compete on teams with a firm no-cut policy. Everyone gets a chance to play. Teams are fielded according to skill levels, and a struggle between junior varsity and C-squad basketball teams is as enthusiastically contested as a varsity clash. Cedar Rapids' schoolgirl athletes compete in nine sports, guided by 144 coaches. Access to training equipment is equal too. The result has been unparalleled athletic success. In the past eight years, Cedar Rapids' boys and girls teams have finished among the state's top three sixty-eight times, winning thirty team championships in ten different sports.

Girls' athletics have become an accustomed part of the way of life in Cedar Rapids. At a recent girls' track meet, runners, shot-putters, hurdlers, high jumpers pitted themselves, one by one, in the age-old contests to run faster, leap higher, throw farther. For many, there were accomplishments they once would have thought impossible. A mile relay team fell into triumphant embrace when word came of qualification for the state finals. Team members shouted the joy of victory—"We did it!"—and then asked permission to break training: "Now can we go to the Dairy Queen, Coach?" Granted.

The mile run was won by seventeen-year-old Julie Nolan of Jefferson High School. Sport is, and will remain, part of her life. "I've been running since the fifth or sixth grade. I want to run in college and then run in marathons." She admires Marathoner Miki Gorman, who ran her fastest when she was in her forties. "That's what I'd like to be doing," she says. Asked if she has been treated differently since she got involved in sports, this once-and-future athlete seemed perplexed: "I don't know, because I've always been an athlete."

Kelly Galliher, fifteen, has grown up in the Cedar Rapids system that celebrates sport for all. The attitudes and resistance that have stunted women's athleticism elsewhere are foreign to Kelly, a sprinter. Does she know that sports are, in some quarters, still viewed as unseemly for young women? "That's ridiculous. Boys sweat, and we're going to sweat. We call it getting out and trying." She has no memories of disapproval from parents or peers. And she has never been called the terrible misnomer that long and unfairly condemned athletic girls. "Tomboy? That idea has gone out here." It's vanishing everywhere.

A Second Look

1. Look carefully at the first four paragraphs. Why are the examples placed in the order they are?

2. Look at the details in these paragraphs. How does the writer make each example seem attractive and special?

3. What is special about the sports program in Cedar Rapids?

4. As you learned in *Looking Forward,* this article was written in 1978. Has the revolution now moved forward or slowed down?

A Cyberlook

One recent charge is that strict enforcement of Title IX will help women's sports programs by weakening men's sports. Review both sides of this argument by looking at recent articles listed under "Education Amendments of 1972" on *InfoTrac College Edition* or locating information using your own browser. Compare your results with those of others in the class. How do you and your classmates feel about this issue?

Ideas for Writing

1. Many public school systems and colleges are faced with shrinking funds for athletics. Should the available money be divided so that a number of sports programs receive support, or should the funds be concentrated in those major programs that are already proven successes? Write a paper in which you take one side of this question or the other. Use as many facts as you can to strengthen your case.

2. In a section of this article not printed here, the author says that through athletic competition children learn lessons about success and failure that will help them later in life. Tell about an experience in which you or someone you know learned such a lesson.

Title IX: Bringing Equality to Athletics

Jacquelyn Gist

Looking Forward

Jackie Gist has long been involved in athletics as a volleyball, softball, and soccer player. Her first love, however, is basketball, which she has played from third grade through college. She was born about the time "Comes the Revolution" was written, and she can see clearly what changes have occurred since Title IX was passed. After reading "Comes the Revolution," Gist wrote her essay, taking her main idea from the last sentence in *Looking Forward:* "As you read, consider what has changed and what has not since the essay first appeared."

Help with Words

mandates *(paragraph 2):* orders, demands
discrepancies *(paragraph 5):* differences, contradictions, variances
enhance *(paragraph 5):* improve, increase

In 1971, a young girl brought a case to the Supreme Court of Connecticut because she was not allowed to participate on the boys' cross-country team even though her high school did not offer a team for women. The judge ruled against her saying, "Athletic competition builds character in our boys. We do not need that kind of character in our girls."

Title IX, which mandates gender equality in all activities sponsored by an educational institution, was passed one year later in 1972. Due to the impact of Title IX, as well as a general change in societal attitudes towards women in athletics, athletic competition has evolved to embrace female athletes in recent years. The WNBA, a professional basketball league for women, is gaining in popularity, and sports such as softball and women's hockey were featured in the 1996 Olympics.

Cheryl Miller, who is considered one of the greatest women of all times to play college basketball, has said: "Without Title IX, I'd be nowhere." Olympic softball player Dot Richardson's story supports that statement as well. Her interest in athletics began prior to the passing of Title IX, when she was denied the opportunity to play Little League baseball because of her gender. The coach saw her playing catch in the park with her brother and was impressed with her skills, yet he told her she could play on the team only if they cut her hair short and called her Bob. In other words, she had to be a boy before she could develop her talents and pursue her dreams. Richardson went on to become a four-time NCAA All-American in softball. The NCAA Player of the Decade for the 1980s, she hit the first home run in Olympic softball history. She is now a doctor in her fourth year of residence as an orthopedic surgeon. Without the passing of Title IX, she would not have been able to attain the status she has today.

The effect of Title IX can also be seen in high school athletics. In 1971, fewer than 300,000 girls participated in interscholastic athletics. However, that number today has swelled to over 2.4 million, and it has become widely acceptable for women to participate in sports. Young girls can be seen on the Little League fields and youth basketball courts of our nation, instead of solely on the sidelines holding pom-poms. College scholarships are available for women in every sport, and girls who participate are rewarded for their hard work rather than being seen as "tomboys." Society is finally starting to accept women's place on athletic fields with open arms.

However, women have not yet reached the same plane as men when it comes to athletic competition. Females are still a few steps behind, and while efforts like Title IX help to bring the genders closer together, equality has not yet been achieved. A study done of NCAA institutions in 1992 showed that gender equity was still a problem. In terms of percentage, females were about 40 points lower than males in respect to participation, athletic scholarships, operating budgets and recruiting budgets. No other department or institution would allow discrepancies such as these in an age when a great emphasis is being placed on women's rights. Because men have historically dominated athletics, however, gender equality in sports is difficult to achieve. Laws such as Title IX are an attempt to bridge that gap and enhance opportunities for women in athletics.

Yet the fact remains that only so much can be done in terms of legality to bring equity to athletics. Laws can mandate anything, but they will not bring about change in society unless the ideals behind the laws are embraced and followed in the hearts of the people. Title IX was a very important step for women in sports, but the values behind the passing of Title IX have had an even stronger impact on society. Those values are the key to completing the evolution of athletic competition. Once a women's place in athletics is established and universally accepted by our society, equality will be embedded in our sense of justice, and laws like Title IX will not be needed. While Title IX is very influential right now, the ultimate goal is to not even need it. When we finally reach a point where we do not need to enforce or can completely eliminate Title IX, then and only then will we honestly be able to say as a society that we have accomplished true gender equity.

A Second Look

1. Jackie Gist opens her essay with a young girl's failure to achieve equality in athletics. Why do you think she starts with this example of failure rather than one of success?

2. According to Gist, why is a change in law not enough to guarantee gender equity in athletics?

3. What are the major divisions in this essay? What transitions does the writer use to move from one major point to the next?

Ideas for Writing

What Jackie Gist says of gender equality is true of equality of any kind: "Laws can mandate anything, but they will not bring about change in society unless the ideals behind the laws are embraced and followed in the hearts of the people." Write an essay discussing what we can do as individuals to help ensure that the ideals behind our laws demanding equality are accepted by the great majority of the American people.

You may wish to write a personal essay, or you may wish to write a more formal "academic" essay, as Gist does. In this kind of paper, you express and support your opinion, but you do not use first person pronouns (I/we). Note that Gist also avoids contractions, slang, sentence fragments, and one- or two-sentence paragraphs. She expresses her opinions, but she does not include personal experiences.

Big, Dumb Jock

Evan Carnes

Looking Forward

In this essay, Evan Carnes, a college football player, looks at the stereotype of the dumb jock. He admits that some student-athletes (especially football players) may contribute to that image without meaning to, but argues that it is unfair to generalize from these examples. Other student-athletes, as Carnes shows, present a very different picture. This essay was written in class.

Three words come to everyone's mind when the label "football player" is cemented to one's name: big, dumb jock. People are reminded of such great football legends as Herschel Walker and the recent college star, Andy Katzenmoyer. Both of these players were untouchable on the playing field, but unreachable in the classroom.

In an interview, Walker totally rewrote the English language, going from past tense to present on the same subject. He then proceeded to make up new verb forms. It really showed Walker's speaking skills! Katzenmoyer didn't do any better. To stay eligible, Katzenmoyer had to take several courses during the summer. His schedule—consisting of music, golf, and a couple of other "cake" courses—yielded a measly 1.5 GPA. He apparently failed at least two of the four classes he took.

These two well-known players, as well as others, have provided examples to support the stereotype that all jocks are dumb. However, many people forget about athletes like Peyton Manning, who graduated in three years with a double major. There's also Champ Baily, who I believe is the most athletic athlete in the NCAA. He's also an athlete in the classroom, pulling a 3.8 GPA.

These and other players have done their part to remove the dumb jock label, yet there are still people out there who don't believe super-star athletes can make it in the classroom.

I am also reminded of all the small-college players who have to succeed in the classroom. The players I mentioned above all had the NFL draft locked by their sophomore years. Class was something that allowed their schools to pay their way to the NFL. But what about the players at small, private colleges? Don't get me wrong. Many of them are great athletes, yet few or none will get the chance at the "league." So what do they have after college football? Jobs. They play football to be able to go to class in order to get those jobs. Football is a love for these guys, and they play it because they don't want to give it up.

Athletes, football players in particular, have long fought through stereotypical prejudices to become what they wanted to become. They bust their butts on the football field, and many bust them just as hard in the classroom. Their work ethic, on and off the field, will allow these particular athletes to make it far in life.

A Second Look

1. Evan Carnes's purpose in this essay is to argue against the stereotype of athletes, especially football players, as big, dumb jocks. What is his writing strategy for doing this? Why does he introduce the negative examples in paragraphs 1 and 2?

2. Several times Carnes uses very informal vocabulary—for example, "cake" courses, measly 1.5 GPA (paragraph 2), bust their butts (paragraph 5). Look for other examples. What does this informal level of language suggest about the writer's intended audience and his plan for writing? Do you think his language is effective? Why or why not?

3. What value does the writer see in playing college football, in spite of its sometimes negative stereotypes?

A Cyberlook

In 1995, Terry Frei, a writer for *The Sporting News*, profiled Jason Reeves, then a math major and senior linebacker at the University of Texas. In "By the Book," Frei introduces us to Reeves as a student-athlete and in diary form takes us through a week of Reeves's campus life. You can read this interesting article by searching "Jason Reeves" on *InfoTrac College Edition*.

Ideas for Writing

Select a stereotypical label that has been applied to you or others you know well and show how that view is a false one. Like Evan Carnes, you need to acknowledge that there may be some truth in the negative view and then show that one cannot generalize from a few individuals to a whole group. In brainstorming, think of as many positive and negative examples as you can, then choose the strongest ones to use in your essay. Organize so that you acknowledge two points of view, but emphasize the one you agree with.

Making Connections

Several of the writers in this unit present quite positive views of sports. Others, such as Arthur Ashe and John Updike, suggest some of the negative aspects. Referring to these selections and using your own knowledge or information you have collected in searching electronic resources, list the pluses and minuses of participation in sports on the amateur level. If your instructor wishes, you may work on this in small groups. Do the positives outweigh the negatives? Can some of the negatives be eliminated or at least neutralized?

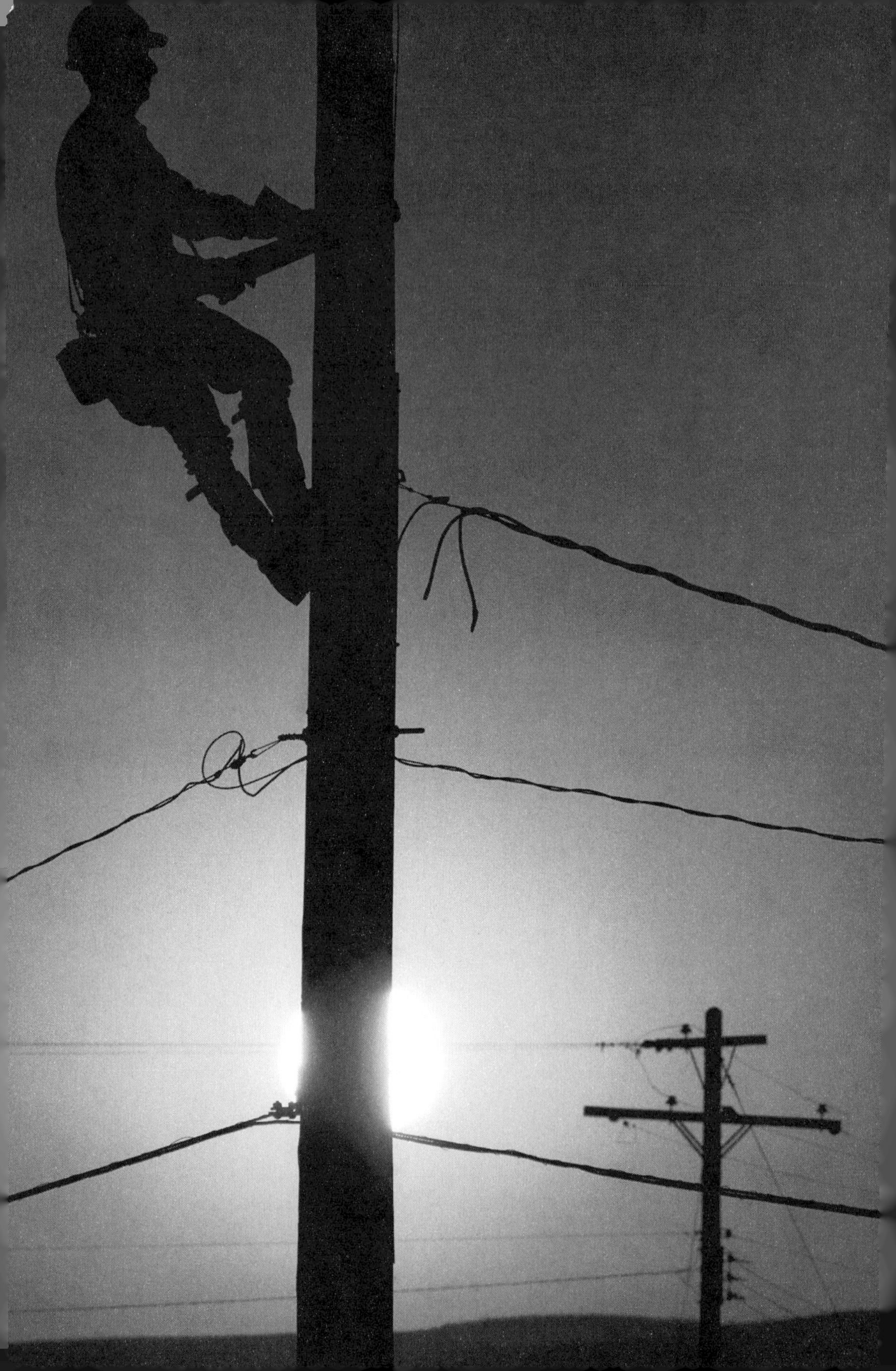

Work

A slightly cynical professor of philosophy once suggested a modern revision of Descartes' famous line: "I earn; therefore, I am." A person's identity and worth, she was suggesting, are often determined by his or her work. Perhaps we dwell so much on our occupations because they consume so much of our time and energy, but many people are certainly focused primarily on their jobs. The essays in this unit give us a look at what it means to work, to overwork, to be out of work, and to be frustrated by work.

The Company Man

Ellen Goodman

Looking Forward

Phil, the subject of Ellen Goodman's essay, is a type frequently seen in many countries, but especially in modern America. He is a "company man": loyal to his employer, dedicated to his job, completely dependable, very hard working, no nonsense. He is, apparently, the perfect employee and an admirable man. But there is one other thing we should know. Goodman tells us in her opening sentence.

Help with Words

obituary *(paragraph 2):* published announcement of a death
coronary thrombosis *(paragraph 2):* heart attack
conceivably *(paragraph 3):* possibly
discreetly *(paragraph 16):* carefully, guardedly

He worked himself to death, finally and precisely, at 3:00 a.m. Sunday morning.

The obituary didn't say that, of course. It said that he died of a coronary thrombosis—I think that was it—but everyone among his friends and acquaintances knew it instantly. He was a perfect Type A, a workaholic, a classic, they said to each other and shook their heads—and thought for five or ten minutes about the way they lived.

This man who worked himself to death finally and precisely at 3:00 a.m. Sunday morning—on his day off—was fifty-one years old and a vice-president. He was, however, one of six vice-presidents, and one of three who might conceivably—if the president died or retired soon enough—have moved to the top spot. Phil knew that.

He worked six days a week, five of them until eight or nine at night, during a time when his own company had begun the four-day week for everyone but the executives. He worked like the Important People. He had no outside "extracurricular interests," unless, of course, you think about a monthly golf game that way. To Phil, it was work. He always ate egg salad sandwiches at his desk. He was, of course, overweight, by 20 or 25 pounds. He thought it was okay, though, because he didn't smoke.

On Saturdays, Phil wore a sports jacket to the office instead of a suit, because it was the weekend.

He had a lot of people working for him, maybe sixty, and most of them liked him most of the time. Three of them will be seriously considered for his job. The obituary didn't mention that.

But it did list his "survivors" quite accurately. He is survived by his wife, Helen, forty-eight years old, a good woman of no particular marketable skills, who worked in an office before marrying and mothering. She had, according to her daughter, given up trying to compete with his work years ago, when the children were small. A company friend said, "I know how much you will miss him." And she answered, "I already have."

"Missing him all these years," she must have given up part of herself which had cared too much for the man. She would be "well taken care of."

His "dearly beloved" eldest of the "dearly beloved" children is a hard-working executive in a manufacturing firm down South. In the day and a half before the funeral, he went around the neighborhood researching his father, asking the neighbors what he was like. They were embarrassed.

His second child is a girl, who is twenty-four and newly married. She lives near her mother and they are close, but whenever she was alone with her father, in a car driving somewhere, they had nothing to say to each other.

The youngest is twenty, a boy, a high-school graduate who has spent the last couple of years, like a lot of his friends, doing enough odd jobs to stay in grass and food. He was the one who tried to grab at his father, and tried to mean enough to him to keep the man at home. He was his father's favorite. Over the last two years, Phil stayed up nights worrying about the boy.

The boy once said, "My father and I only board here."

At the funeral, the sixty-year-old company president told the forty-eight-year-old widow that the fifty-one-year-old deceased had meant much to the company and would be missed and would be hard to replace. The widow didn't look him in the eye. She was afraid he would read her bitterness and, after all, she would need him to straighten out the finances — the stock options and all that.

Phil was overweight and nervous and worked too hard. If he wasn't at the office, he was worried about it. Phil was a Type A, a heart-attack natural. You could have picked him out in a minute from a lineup.

So when he finally worked himself to death, at precisely 3:00 a.m. Sunday morning, no one was really surprised.

By 5:00 p.m. the afternoon of the funeral, the company president had begun, discreetly of course, with care and taste, to make inquiries about his replacement. One of three men. He asked around: "Who's been working the hardest?"

A Second Look

1. What specific details in Goodman's essay show that Phil was a good "company man"?

2. What effects have Phil's work habits had on each of the other members of his family? Be specific.

3. What is the company's attitude toward the death of its "man"?

4. Why does Goodman use the kinds of detail we find in paragraph 13? What does she suggest about these people?

5. One of Goodman's major points — probably the most important one — is never stated directly; it is implied or suggested by the whole essay. What do you think it is?

A Cyberlook

1. Not everyone agrees on the effects of overwork on the worker's life and family relationships. Access *InfoTrac College Edition* and search under "workaholism" to find articles that express different views on the subject.

2. Our tendency to overwork has generated a great amount of material on the Internet. One popular search engine has almost 3,000 listings under "workaholics." Search this term with one or more browsers and note the variety of information in various forms—print, art, advertising, and others—and in several languages. You may even come across an organization named Workaholics Anonymous. Check out several sites of various kinds and compare your findings with those of other classmates. (But do not trade your addiction to work for an addiction to the Internet.)

Ideas for Writing

1. You may know a company man or company woman. If so, describe this person. Tell your readers (who do not know your subject) about his or her work habits, personal habits, family relationships, and so forth. What do you think drives this person to be a workaholic?

2. Write an obituary for yourself, the kind you hope will appear when you are gone—many years from now. Give the newspaper readers information about your age, work, religious or social affiliations, survivors, whatever you want to be recorded and remembered.

Blue-Collar Journal: A College President's Sabbatical

John R. Coleman

Looking Forward

In the spring of 1973, John R. Coleman—then President of Haverford College, a noted economist, and chair of the board of directors of the Federal Reserve Bank of Philadelphia—asked for and received a sabbatical, an academic leave with pay. He told few people of his plans. For eight weeks, President John Coleman became plain Jack Coleman, common laborer. Traveling about, Coleman was (among other things) a sewer-line construction worker, a dish washer, and a trash collector. During this time, he kept a journal of his activities. The following entry was made while Coleman was working as a salad man at the Union Oyster House in Boston.

Help with Words

blitz *(paragraph 4):* a sudden, heavy military offensive
forage *(paragraph 13):* hunt or scavenge for food
respite *(paragraph 13):* rest, relief
fray *(paragraph 28):* battle

Sunday, March 18

I would feel cheated if I had lived out my life without experiencing a day like today.

Saturday's crowds or poor inventory policy or a combination of the two left us short of almost everything today except for the seafood itself. On Sunday there is no way to get new stocks. We must wait until the markets open on Monday morning.

In spite of radio warnings of snow, the dining rooms were packed from 1:00 until 9:00. The first sign that we were in trouble came about 2:00. The early warning came from the cherry tomatoes. One of them goes in each of the tossed salads, and one of the tossed salads goes with almost every plate of food. The crisis atmosphere generated by the news that there were no more tomatoes so early in the day was startling. Shock on all sides. But that event was followed hard by the news that the cucumbers had also given out. A slice of them goes in each salad too.

Now it was like moving into blitz conditions in wartime.

"What are we supposed to do?" one of the waitresses moaned. "Tossed salads always have a tomato and a piece of cucumber." I saw almost 150 years of Oyster House history being swept away in one evening.

"We'll just make do without them," another said. She was the type who sang "There'll Always Be an England" in London's air-raid shelters in 1943.

"But we can't serve just plain lettuce," the first one sighed.

Fortunately, that possibility was soon removed. The cut salad greens ran out about 4:00. We had had only four or five plastic bags of them to start the day, and that was nowhere near enough. Rationing the dwindling stock had failed dismally; no waitress was going to give her customers less than a full bowl of greens. But we still had a substitute: we could fall back on chopping up the two cases of whole lettuce that lay on the cooler's shelves.

I chopped up the heads and washed them as fast as I could, all the while trying to keep up with the sandwich orders coming in.

"We're out of salad," each new waitress coming on duty called out. That was like calling the civil defense office to alert them that the enemy was coming while the volunteers there were fighting a pitched battle in the headquarters yard itself.

"I know already," I called out from the cutting table in the back.

I cut not only the lettuce but my hand as well. Band-Aids didn't stem the flow of blood as fast as I thought they would. I wondered when the first-aid corps would come by.

The last piece of the newly chopped lettuce went into the dining room about 6:30. We then brought in reinforcements: the assistant manager went out to see what he could forage from other restaurants in the area. They were under attack too, and eight heads were all they could spare. That brought us half an hour of respite. I combed the garbage for some outer leaves that I had rejected earlier as being below the house standard. They were pressed into service now. I think I even washed them first.

Meanwhile, there was news of fresh disasters. The strawberry shortcake gave out for a full two hours, until the chef was able to bake more. One waitress in that period managed to sell a customer a shortcake using cornbread as the base. I hoped someone would cite her later for exceptional service under fire.

The Boston cream pie ran out about 6:00. The whole wheat bread and the rye went at about the same time. The stock of sour-cream cups and whipping cream had disappeared while I was chopping lettuce, and there was a long period before I got around to fixing more.

The dinner noise got louder.

"Two chicken club sandwiches, no mayonnaise on one."

"There's no butterscotch pudding here."

"Could you just slice one tomato for a customer who insists on a salad?"

"Toast for Newburg."

"Give me a deluxe shrimp cocktail. But take your time—the old goat can wait."

"I know you're busy, but can you open this fruit salad jar?"

"A lady says the crab tastes funny."

"Is there any more gingerbread?"

"Half a grapefruit."

"Where's my crabmeat salad? Who's the bitch that picked it up?"

One good thing was that, once we ran out of salad greens, no one but me knew we were out of French dressing too.

And so it went all evening long. Surprisingly, no one suffered much shock once that first terrible news about the cherry tomatoes had sunk in. It was chins up and into the fray from then on.

I had been wondering what the assistant manager does besides look stern, unlock the lobster safe, and borrow lettuce. I found out in the midst of the panic that he was the one to whom I should report that the seat in the men's toilet had fallen off. (I forget how I had time to discover that casualty.)

It was a cold and clear night when I came out at 9:45. There was a full moon over the plaza. The promised snow hadn't amounted to anything at all. But the square was empty just the same. We had met the enemy, and they had run.

👁 A Second Look

1. Coleman gives an amusing and realistic picture of several fast-paced hours in the kitchen of the Union Oyster House. What are some of the techniques he uses to bring this scene to life for his readers?

2. Coleman describes the 1:00 to 9:00 shift as if it were a battle in which the action ebbs and flows. Pick out some of the words and phrases he uses to give this impression.

3. Why does Coleman say: "I would feel cheated if I had lived out my life without experiencing a day like today" (paragraph 1)?

4. When Coleman went to work at the Union Oyster House, he worried that friends or former students living in Boston might recognize him. In fact, none of the customers paid any attention to him. "At the college," he wrote in another entry, "I have become accustomed to being noticed when I walk into a room." But Jack Coleman the salad man went unrecognized: "Probably . . . my uniform is the best disguise I could have." What does this suggest about people and the jobs they hold?

A Cyberlook

John Coleman notes with surprise that, dressed in his kitchen worker's uniform, he becomes almost invisible; he seems to be nobody. This is an experience shared by many workers in low-paying jobs that require little education, workers who may feel they are denied dignity and respect. The problem is often magnified if the workers are recent immigrants to the United States. Yet these low-paying service industry jobs are on the rise, increasing the number of workers who feel undervalued or ignored. For recent research on this topic, search for Richard Rothstein, "RAND Report on Immigrant Education" (1996). If you have difficulty finding the site, go to the *Wadsworth Developmental English* web page and click on Textbook Resource Centers.

Ideas for Writing

Describe an interesting day (or part of a day) at a job you have held. Show the reader what the job is really like. Describe the people with whom you are working. Tell how they interact. Use interesting details and active language so that the workplace comes alive for the reader, just as the kitchen of the Union Oyster House does.

As before, begin by listing everything you can think of about the job, the people, the particular day you are going to describe. Then go through this material, determining what is useful and what is not. You might arrange your essay chronologically. You should also consider focusing on the place where you work (how it is laid out) or on the people. Choose the pattern of organization you think will make your workday most interesting to your readers.

Out of Work in America

Roger Rosenblatt

Looking Forward

The severe recession that began in 1990 was only one of a series of economic downturns occurring over several decades. Each time the economy slips, many Americans lose their jobs. At the end of the decade, the United States enjoyed great economic growth, but shifts in employment patterns and corporate downsizing still put many Americans out of work. As Roger Rosenblatt points out, financial hardship is only part of what the unemployed suffer. Even worse, perhaps, is the loss of self-esteem.

Help with Words

unctuous *(paragraph 1):* seemingly, but not actually, sincere and concerned (literally, oily or greasy)
incompetence *(paragraph 2):* inability, inadequacy
debacles *(paragraph 5):* terrible failures, downfalls
guinea *(paragraph 7):* a British gold coin (no longer in use)
exude *(paragraph 8):* send out, emit, radiate
inept *(paragraph 11):* awkward, unable to perform satisfactorily
chronically *(paragraph 11):* occurring for a long period of time
sedition *(paragraph 11):* disloyalty, treachery
expelled *(paragraph 13):* cast out

Only once has the scene been portrayed realistically, and that was in the movie *Broadcast News*. The news division of the TV network in the movie is firing employees wholesale. One man, who has worked there forever, is told by his unctuous boss: "Now, if there's anything I can do for you." The ex-employee responds with equal warmth: "Well, I certainly hope you die soon."

He might have added, "slowly and with severe pain," but the sentiments were implied. The fury at being fired not for incompetence but so that a company can cut costs is wild and deep. Soon it turns on itself like a maddened animal. Eventually, if there is no new job at hand, anger flattens out to a sense of helplessness, then to rattling self-doubt, and finally takes the form of gazing into space.

People all over America are running through such emotions these days. Since the recession was declared official in July 1990, 1.4 million unemployed have been added to the rolls. In May the unemployment rate increased from 6.6 percent to 6.9 percent. The out-of-work now total 8.6 million, which does not include 5.9 million who work part-time but seek full-time jobs.

These people have become words in the news, the casualties of "layoffs" and "cutbacks." Some are "involuntary part-timers." All have been tossed out of the work that they know and that they do best.

The companies that are doing the tossing are sometimes to blame, sometimes not. A few places have been forced to decrease staffs because of the junk bond and S&L debacles. Some others are belatedly paying penalties for overstaffing and thoughtless management. Most are simply corporate victims of hard times.

For the people who have been laid off, the results are the same: They have become exiles in their own country, isolated from friends, neighbors, their pasts, their senses of purpose and self—cast out of America's history and future.

To be out of a job in America is like a special punishment of the gods, two gods in particular: money and work. The feelings of safety and social stature that come from having money are not peculiarly American. Lord Byron once wrote a friend: "They say that knowledge is power. I used to think so, but I now know that they meant money. . . . Every guinea is a philosopher's stone. . . . Cash is virtue." If one turns to the Bible for another, more spiritual view, there's no help in Ecclesiastes: "Wine maketh merry: but money answereth all things."

Work, however, is the national engine, the way America recognizes itself. The sense of forcefulness that the country likes to exude is connected to labor, and labor to character. One seeks "honest work." The kid who gets a paper route or who splits rails and grows up to be President embraces a national destiny 225 years old, even older.

America, in the beginning, had to be made, and that took work. Since every individual American is taught to be self-made, that too takes work. You are a product of your own labors. You are what you do.

When a man or a woman is deprived of work, then, the feeling of isolation is overwhelming. Exile is sometimes a precondition for clear-sightedness or superiority of vision, but not in the case of the out-of-work in America. They may view their country more clearly, but what they learn is how closely tied they have been to their country's nature and will. One moment they are swimming in the national current, the next they are strangers to themselves.

One reason, I think, that America has been so inept at helping the chronically out-of-work is that there is a national resentment toward those who cannot hack it. It's not that Americans resist the idea of welfare because they dread big government; given other contexts, such as social security, they adore big government. But they see joblessness as a kind of crime or sin, an act of sedition. When politicians speak of getting people off public assistance and back on the job, it always sounds like a moral lecture. The lesson is: Idleness is un-American.

I think of the man in *Broadcast News* as a real person, male or female, and I wonder how he is doing. If he's lucky, he has a pension after his long years of service or a nest egg somewhere. Even so, he has been separated from his country and from himself by that news division which, as if engaging in deliberate cruelty, sends him televised reports on how the economy continues to shrink, and how many more like him are made castaways.

Each new day opens to him full of bright and empty air. He has been expelled by the New World, and he searches for another. But there is no other.

A Second Look

1. This essay is primarily an analysis of a situation and an expression of the writer's opinion. How does he support that opinion?

2. Overall, how does Rosenblatt organize the essay? List his major points. How does he move from one to another?

3. Rosenblatt says of those who have been laid off: "They have become exiles in their own country, isolated from friends, neighbors, their pasts, their senses of purpose and self—cast out of America's history and future" (paragraph 6). Explain why they feel this way.

4. According to the author, why has America done such a poor job of helping the long-term unemployed?

A Cyberlook

1. To get an idea of the great concern Americans have about losing jobs, getting hired again, and coping with unemployment, search the Internet using terms such as "downsizing," "job loss," or "layoffs." You will find thousands of entries. Sample a few of these and compare your results with those of your classmates. Do you find some common trends among these many discussions of unemployment?

2. For a first-person narrative of a man who was forced into early retirement after nearly 25 years with the same company, access *InfoTrac College Edition,* search under "job loss" and read Robert B. Murray, "Downsizing Hits Home."

Ideas for Writing

Some say that Americans are particularly likely to judge others according to their work; in effect, they believe that "you are what you do." Do you believe that we tend to judge others in this way, or do we look more closely at the person than at the work he or she does? Write an essay expressing your opinion and giving specific examples to support it. If you can give examples from personal experience, that is particularly strong support.

Working Mothers

Janet Krebs

Looking Forward

When it comes to the subject of working mothers, Janet Krebs speaks with authority. A secretary, mother of four, and a college student, Krebs has had years of experience with the inflexibility of the business world and the tendency of male managers to react to the special needs of working mothers with indifference or even hostility. In her essay, she examines this problem and offers some specific solutions.

Help with Words

arrogance *(paragraph 2):* feelings of superiority
insinuate *(paragraph 2):* hint, imply
culmination *(paragraph 2):* climax
elegantly *(paragraph 3):* beautifully, richly
alleviate *(paragraph 5):* ease, make less difficult

The number of working mothers has more than doubled since the 1950s, with the majority of families needing two incomes in order to mount a halfway decent battle against ever-rising expenses. Women joining the work force may help the family finances, but this increased female presence also creates a need to redefine the corporate world as men know it.

I have been a secretary for many years and have been harassed about a parent-teacher conference done on my lunch hour and doctor's appointments when my children were sick. I have been expected to miss every awards banquet or ceremony that my children were in because these were scheduled during business hours. To add insult to injury, I was recently interviewed for a higher level secretarial position within the company. The interview was going well until one particular high-level manager had the egotistical arrogance to insinuate that my having four children would cause me to miss work, which would cause me to fall behind in my duties. I was being discriminated against because I chose to have children. Had I been with this company longer than three months, I might have pointed this out; instead, I kept my mouth shut and went back to my desk—fuming, steam pouring out my ears. This incident was the culmination of a series of hassles and harassment simply because I have to work and chose to have children.

In a male-dominated world, women have to do everything better and faster just to get what we hope is corporate equality. The worst part in juggling motherhood and my fight for corporate equality is seeing the disappointment on my children's faces because I'm not there when they need me, or just when I should be. Why should working women have to slight their children's daily needs in order to have a successful career? Men can be fathers and still rise to the highest levels of corporate success. Why can't women do the same? After all, we all start out with that same elegantly designed piece of paper signifying our Ph.D. or M.B.A. or B.A. degree in political science, communications, or physics—degrees we worked equally hard for. The difference is that when men enter into a male-dominant work force, it is structured specifically for them; but when women enter, we're like aliens with baggage, tolerated but not accepted.

In a way, we're almost repeating history. We're fighting the same battle our grandmothers and great-grandmothers fought in the early 1900s. Women won their right to vote and be looked upon as equal in every place but the work force, a battle we have really just begun to fight. We are intelligent, educated members of the human race, capable of handling corporate responsibility and motherhood. As we, one by precious one, make it to the corporate executive level, we slowly near the end of a time-consuming and needless battle for equality, as we continue to prove our self-worth.

I have noticed that men who on occasion help with their own children tend to be more understanding of our struggle with career and motherhood. Perhaps influenced by them, some companies have developed flex time to help alleviate some of the stress of managing our personal responsibilities along with our corporate ones. This works extremely well, provided we have an enlightened boss.

Between flex time and the fact that more and more men are hard pressed to finally help carry the burden of family and career, many working mothers agree there is light at the end of the tunnel. As we march onward, we hope that the only knowledge of corporate inequality our granddaughters will have will be the courageous battle stories we'll tell of how we achieved our individual victories.

A Second Look

1. It is important for someone writing a persuasive essay to establish a *persona,* an image of what the writer is like and what he or she knows about the subject. How would you describe Janet Krebs's persona? How does she create it?

2. According to the author, what positive steps can companies take to help their female employees who have children? What may help such companies to achieve corporate equality more quickly?

3. Krebs does not acknowledge that there is another "side" to this issue. Are there, in fact, reasons why working mothers might not be as reliable and productive as working women without children or, perhaps, as men? If your instructor wishes, you may hold an informal debate on this issue in class.

A Cyberlook

1. Working mothers is another of those hot-button topics that is popular with Internet surfers. Visit several sites to see what some of the sub-issues are and how people on opposing sides argue their points of view. Compare your results with those of your classmates.

2. Two recent books on this topic have attracted a good bit of attention. One, *Not Guilty: The Good News About Working Mothers* (Scribner, 1998) is by Betty Holcomb, an editor at *Working Mother* magazine. The other, by

Susan Chira, an editor at *The New York Times*, is entitled, *A Mother's Place: Taking the Debate About Working Mothers Beyond Guilt and Blame* (Harper-Collins, 1998). You can read reviews of these books on *InfoTrac College Edition*. Search under "working mothers" or try an advanced search by clicking on *PowerTrac*, then clicking Author Index and entering the author's names.

3 For a look at major issues concerning all women in the work place, especially those at non-managerial levels, you can visit Working Women Working Together, a site maintained by the AFL-CIO. If you have difficulty finding the site, go to the *Wadsworth Developmental English* web page and click on Textbook Resource Centers.

Ideas for Writing

For many corporate managers, the issue of working mothers finally comes down to efficiency and profit. Many managers feel (though they will rarely say so publicly) that working mothers are not as reliable, not as focused, and ultimately not as productive as other workers. Do these managers have a valid point, or are they simply being influenced by stereotypical thinking? Using experiences from your own family, the class discussion of question 3 in *A Second Look,* and the results of your Internet and *InfoTrac* searches, write a paper supporting one side of this argument. If your instructor wishes, you can discuss the topic (and perhaps even write the arguments) in pro and con groups.

Making Connections

Ellen Goodman and Roger Rosenblatt look at examples of the negative or destructive aspects of work. John R. Coleman sees primarily the positive side. How are the examples described by Goodman and Rosenblatt different from those described by Coleman? Considering the people described in the essays, what sort of general statement could you make about the varying attitudes toward work and self?

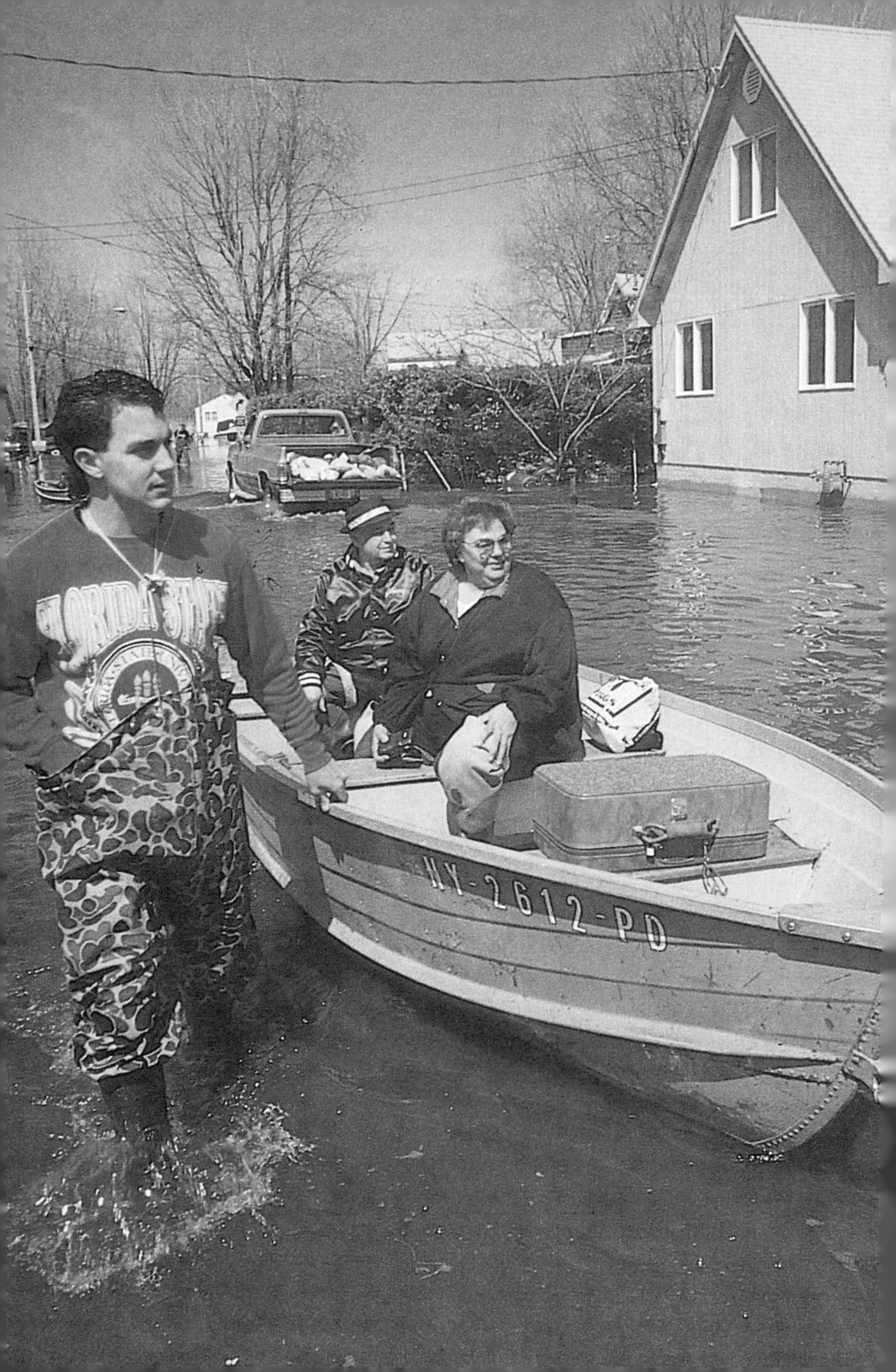
NY-2612-PD

Heroism

Every age has its heroes, but over the centuries our standards for heroism have changed. Today many people feel that heroism is no longer possible, but the writers in this unit disagree. Some of the heroes described, like those of older times, are recognized for their heroic deeds. Others may blend in with the crowd of ordinary people, but they are there, standing up for what they believe is right and sacrificing for the sake of others.

Where Have All the Heroes Gone?

Pete Axthelm

Looking Forward

In this essay about heroism, Pete Axthelm not only identifies heroes from the past; he also considers whether our modern society is capable of producing twentieth-century heroes. He points out that most Americans are suspicious of courageous deeds and that the media are fast to expose any flaws of so-called heroes. Nevertheless, Americans still respect heroism and admire bravery and daring whenever they find true examples of it.

Help with Words

unabashed *(paragraph 2):* unashamed, unembarrassed
carping *(paragraph 2):* finding fault
martial *(paragraph 2):* warlike
alleged *(paragraph 2):* assumed but not proven
technocrats *(paragraph 2):* specialists in technology
scrutinize *(paragraph 3):* look closely at
barrage *(paragraph 3):* heavy artillery fire; here, a prolonged attack of words and accusations
bureaucrats *(paragraph 4):* officials who follow routine
legions *(paragraph 4):* large groups
prattle *(paragraph 4):* talk foolishly
elusive *(paragraph 5):* hard to define
chic *(paragraph 6):* fashionable

segment *(paragraph 6):* a part
artifacts *(paragraph 7):* man-made objects, especially very old ones
reputedly *(paragraph 7):* according to popular belief
stark *(paragraph 7):* extremely simple
idiom *(paragraph 11):* a style of speaking

Be Silent, Friend
Here Heroes Died
To Blaze a Trail
For Other Men

Near that sign at the door of the Alamo, there are several simpler warnings. NO SMOKING. QUIET. GENTLEMEN REMOVE HATS. I did not see anyone light up inside the Alamo. There were few noises except for the subdued and reverent words of the tour guides. The gentlemen were all bareheaded. And somehow these minor gestures of respect seemed important. Standing in the dusty courtyard in the dry Texas heat, in a season when Americans were knifing one another over tanks of gasoline, I felt refreshed to be in a place where the memory of heroism and trailblazing can still make a friend take off his hat.

I have been reading quite a bit lately about how America has grown too rich, too confused, or too sophisticated for heroes. John Wayne is gone, his larger-than-life adventures replaced mainly by movies that offer only blinding special effects or characters trying to find themselves. Even when a rare film like "The Deer Hunter" attempts to portray an unabashed war hero, nobody notices: The critical reaction is mainly carping about its martial philosophy or alleged racism. Sports stars, once expected to embody heroism as well as talent, have lost much of their luster and our trust in a flurry of team-hopping and renegotiation of contracts. The astronauts have been smugly dismissed as technocrats, their heritage reduced to a nervous summer of Skylab jokes. Once, we routinely asked our kids who their heroes were. Today we fumble for answers when they ask us if there are any heroes left.

Vietnam and Watergate played their part in all this, as we learned to beware our leaders and to scrutinize them, warts and all. The media have done so with a vengeance, and few leaders can stand up to the barrage. But a cynical age now accepts the tarnished coin of celebrity in place of heroic virtue—and thus the best-seller lists are filled with books by Watergate felons and their co-conspirators.

Destiny: I am not convinced of the impossibility of modern heroism. Anyone who has met the coal miners of eastern Kentucky or the firemen of the South Bronx would be foolish to proclaim the death of self-sacrifice or bravery—qualities that surely have some relation to heroism. Can an era be hopelessly bleak and unheroic when two young journalists can help to bring down a corrupt administration and a few bureaucrats stand up to expose the waste and carelessness of the bureaucracies that they serve? Even in a troubled land of cookie-cutter shopping malls and thought-deadening discos, I suspect there are a few people who still seek out the lonely roads, take the personal risks and dare to shape their world. While modern legions may prattle about human potential, those few actually fulfill it. And call it destiny.

Before trying to define or search for heroism, I wanted to reach out and touch that elusive quality. Surely men touched it at Valley Forge or San Juan Hill, on the Bad Lands of the frontier or the Sea of Tranquility. But few felt it on more intimate terms than the Texas freedom fighters of the 1830s. So the Alamo seemed as good a place as any to make a start.

Some visitors have been disappointed by this small, modest shrine in the midst of downtown San Antonio. Today, the Alamo must battle for tourists' attention against the chic Riverwalk and teeming streets nearby. On a corner a block away, for example, a large sign over a servicemen's Christian center proclaims: RIGHTEOUSNESS EXALTETH A NATION. I did not see any servicemen in the center as I passed. But at night, a segment of the city's large hooker population works that corner. I asked one girl there about the Alamo. "I'm from Miami, what do I know about that crap?" she said. "You ain't another one of those John Wayne freaks, are you?" An unpromising backdrop for history.

But the Alamo overcomes. In its resistance to the vast scale of Texas, it asserts a stubborn grandeur of its own. Its artifacts are simple, its tone understated. In one display case is a rifle with which Davy Crockett reputedly killed 350 bears in one summer. "That's only a legend, of course," tour guide Lupe Nava warns softly. "But Crockett was such a good marksman that it could be true." The heroes, Crockett and Jim Bowie and commanding officer William Travis and the rest, are never oversold here. In merciful contrast to the stars of our modern tourist attractions, they are never depicted in life-size "multimedia presentations" that can only serve to cut the subjects down to size. Their story is stark, their memory vivid on its own terms. I think there are some lessons in this. . . .

An independent Republic of Texas was what the heroes of the Alamo wanted. The price was their lives, and the odds against them were about 30 to 1. They knew the odds and played out the deadly game. But they fought so bravely that Santa Anna's huge Mexican Army was weakened. Forty-six days after the fall of the Alamo in 1836, another Texas army routed the Mexicans at San Jacinto. The Alamo had been remembered and avenged, and Texas was free. In death, the heroes of the Alamo had reshaped their world. In doing so, they had taken a fierce self-respect to the level of heroism—and provided a working definition that endures and illuminates.

Some comparisons are irresistible. Jim Bowie, among the oldest Alamo fighters at forty-one, was a wealthy landowner with connections in high places. Today, when the lower classes do our fighting and wealth and connections smooth many a journey through politics or business, it may be hard to grasp the ideals that drove Bowie to the Texas war—and kept him there even after he was stricken with typhoid pneumonia. Bowie died, his famous knife bloodied, while fighting from his sickbed. . . .

James Butler Bonham was a courier who left the Alamo during the siege and rode to Goliad, ninety-five miles away, to plead for reinforcement. He is less known than Crockett or Bowie, but his horse, it seems to me, should gallop through our modern consciousness. . . . The commander at Goliad could offer no troops. At that moment, Bonham knew that the Alamo was doomed. But he turned around, fought his way back through the Mexican Army and rejoined his comrades to fight to a certain death.

Challenge: No one faced the odds more squarely than Bonham. No one had more options. Already a hero, he could have joined other Texas forces, fought to other glories, grabbed a few more days or years for a life that ended at twenty-nine. In the modern idiom that replaces self-respect with self-serving, he could have coped. It is difficult even to speculate on the depths of Bonham's dedication. Perhaps modern analysts would speak of obsession, self-destructive tendencies, [or] male bonding among heroes. But the hoofbeats of Bonham's ride express it much better. They leave us with the lingering and essential challenge: Who among modern heroes would have made that return trip? . . .

Human Nature: On my way home from the Alamo, I stopped in Nashville to talk with songwriter Tom T. Hall, whose country music salutes countless everyday heroes. "I think that heroism is basic to human nature," Hall said. "We look at Martin Luther King or the Pope going into Communist Poland, and we can't really avoid the possibilities of heroism. Maybe our own kind takes a much smaller form, like going into a mine shaft every morning or making the refrigerator payments in time to keep a family eating. But it's there. Given the chance, I think a lot of guys in mines or factories would make that ride back into the Alamo."

Those words may be hard to believe. But to stop believing them would be like smoking in the Alamo. To deny modern heroism, it seems to me, is to admit that the odds are too long, the game no longer worth playing. Without heroes, we lose something of ourselves. I do not believe that we will ever accept that loss without listening one more time for hoofbeats.

A Second Look

1. What typical sources of heroism does Axthelm mention in paragraph 2? Why are these heroes no longer acceptable?

2. In what ways did the Vietnam War and the Watergate scandal influence Americans' attitudes toward heroes?

3. To many current students, Vietnam and Watergate seem like ancient history. But what of recent events involving President Clinton and Whitehouse intern Monica Lewinsky? Did this long-running scandal further erode our belief in heroes? Have we developed an even greater tendency to "beware our leaders and to scrutinize them, warts and all"?

166 *Heroism*

4. Axthelm singles out James Butler Bonham for special notice. Why should Bonham be considered more courageous than the other fighters at the Alamo?

5. In explaining Bonham's options, Axthelm says, "he could have coped." What does the popular word *coped* mean in this sentence?

6. Why does Axthelm frequently mention the hoofbeats of Bonham's horse? (See paragraphs 10, 11, and 13.)

7. Review the characteristics of the Alamo fighters mentioned in paragraph 8, and then write the definition of heroism that this paragraph suggests.

A Cyberlook

1. The seige of the Alamo, which lasted from 24 February to 6 March 1836, is not merely history. It has become the subject for legend, songs, and films. But this is the popular, majority view. Many Americans, especially those of Hispanic descent, see the Battle of the Alamo and the whole war with Mexico in a different light. For a look at the old and new interpretations of the Alamo experience, see Tod Olson, "Remember the Alamo! (But how?)" on *InfoTrac College Edition*. Search "Alamo."

2. Whether or not most people now believe in heroes, we use the word to describe a remarkable range of individuals from athletes Tara Lipinski and Mark McGwire to brave Cub Scouts to winners of the Congressional Medal of Honor and even to characters in DC Comics. Using *InfoTrac College Edition* or any of the popular Internet search engines, collect the names of a number of people (real or imaginary) currently described as heroes. Compare your results with those of your classmates. What are the common characteristics that cause these individuals to be designated modern heroes? Discuss this question in small groups. If your instructor wishes, groups can use these examples to write a brief report on the meaning of the term *hero* as we enter the twenty-first century.

Ideas for Writing

"Anyone who has met the coal miners of eastern Kentucky or the firemen of the South Bronx," Pete Axthelm writes, "would be foolish to proclaim the death of self-sacrifice or bravery—qualities that surely have some relation to heroism." Using Axthelm's criteria—self-sacrifice and/or bravery—write about a person whom you consider a hero. This may be a well-known or unknown person, and the term hero may certainly refer to either gender. If you select a person who is not well known, be sure to explain clearly to the reader exactly who your hero is and what he or she has done. Also be certain to explain how this individual has exhibited self-sacrifice and/or bravery, terms that you may wish to define in your own way.

Note: Before you write, you may want to read the next selection, a student essay written on this topic.

A Personal Hero

Bethany Hampton

Looking Forward

In this essay, written in class, student Beth Hampton is responding to the prompt that follows Pete Axthelm's essay, "Where Have All the Heroes Gone?" (See page 161.) She tells us that reading Axthelm has changed her view of heroes and reminded her that they can be found very nearby, even in her own family.

Help with Words

black lung *(paragraph 4):* a slow-developing, fatal lung disease caused by breathing in coal dust over a long period of time; medically, pneumoconiosis
lethal *(paragraph 4):* deadly, fatal

Pete Axthelm has stated in a *Newsweek* essay that, even in the late twentieth century, heroism is still possible. "Anyone who has met the coal miners of eastern Kentucky or the firemen of the South Bronx," he writes, "would be foolish to proclaim the death of self-sacrifice or bravery—qualities that surely have some relation to heroism." When asked in the past who my hero is, I have responded with someone I admire and know quite well—my Sunday School teacher. But as I read Axthelm's statement, a different person came to mind. That person is my great-grandfather, Odie Ritchie.

Marrying at age seventeen and starting a family right away was nothing uncommon in the 1930s. Neither was working as a coal miner if you lived in the mountains of eastern Kentucky. Each and every day, Grandaddy would go to the mines and work endless hours to support his wife and what would eventually be nine children. When he returned home from work each day, he made sure that his farm was properly maintained. After that, he sometimes had to work on a neighboring farm to earn a few extra dollars.

He exhibited self-sacrifice in many aspects of his life. He sacrificed sleep, food, time with his family, and his health so that he could provide for his wife and children and make them happy. I have heard many stories of how he would go without meals so that all of the children could eat.

My great-grandfather was also a very brave man. After years of working in a mine, he developed a disease common to coal miners, black lung. He fought this lethal disease for several years before being permanently hospitalized. During his hospitalization, my grandmother wrote a letter to his favorite country singer, Loretta Lynn, and told her of his struggles, sacrifices, bravery, fabulous personality, and generous nature. When Ms. Lynn received the letter, she called and said she would be at the hospital as soon as possible. Within a few hours, she walked through the door of his room, and for the last time he smiled a gorgeous smile. Ms. Lynn prayed with him and assured him that it was okay to let go. This courageous man had never given in to anything in his life, but for once he had no control.

Through his struggles, sacrifices, and bravery, Odie Ritchie became a hero in many people's eyes, including mine. Each day I look at the photograph of him and Loretta Lynn and wish I could have known him longer. To me, he truly is a hero.

A Second Look

1. Some student writers, especially when they are working in class with the pressure of a time limit, have trouble focusing on an assigned topic and not wandering away to a related subject. How does Beth Hampton show that she remains focused on the assignment?

2. What specific details does Hampton use to demonstrate that her great-grandfather exhibited the heroic qualities of self-sacrifice and bravery?

3. One of the reasons this is an interesting and successful paper is the variety of sentence structure. Reread paragraphs 1 and 2 and examine the ways in which the writer alters the usual subject-verb or subject-verb-object structure.

I Know Why the Caged Bird Sings

Maya Angelou

Looking Forward

Maya Angelou has established a wide reputation as a singer and actress as well as a writer and teacher. In this chapter from her autobiography, Angelou recalls the suspense and excitement in a small town in Arkansas over Joe Louis's match to keep the title of world heavyweight champion. Notice the ways in which Angelou shows the reader the importance of the match before she states this main idea directly.

Help with Words

apprehensive *(paragraph 2):* fearful
cracker *(paragraph 3):* slang for a white person
assent *(paragraph 10):* approval
"master's voice" *(paragraph 12):* part of an advertising slogan for RCA radios and phonographs
maimed *(paragraph 16):* wounded or crippled
accusations *(paragraph 17):* charges
ordained *(paragraph 17):* divinely ordered
hewers *(paragraph 17):* cutters
ambrosia *(paragraph 27):* food for the gods
white lightning *(paragraph 27):* moonshine, homemade whiskey

The last inch of space was filled, yet people continued to wedge themselves along the walls of the Store. Uncle Willie had turned the radio up to its last notch so that youngsters on the porch wouldn't miss a word. Women sat on kitchen chairs, dining room chairs, stools and upturned wooden boxes. Small children and babies perched on every lap available and men leaned on the shelves or each other.

The apprehensive mood was shot through with shafts of gaiety, as a black sky is streaked with lightning.

"I ain't worried 'bout this fight. Joe's gonna whip that cracker like it's open season."

"He gone whip him till that white boy call him Momma."

At last the talking was finished and the string-along songs about razor blades were over and the fight began.

"A quick jab to the head." In the Store the crowd grunted. "A left to the head and a right and another left." One of the listeners cackled like a hen and was quieted.

"They're in a clench, Louis is trying to fight his way out."

Some bitter comedian on the porch said, "That white man don't mind hugging that niggah now, I betcha."

"The referee is moving in to break them up, but Louis finally pushed the contender away and it's an uppercut to the chin. The contender is hanging on, now he's backing away. Louis catches him with a short left to the jaw."

A tide of murmuring assent poured out the doors and into the yard.

"Another left and another left. Louis is saving that mighty right. . . ." The mutter in the Store had grown into a baby roar and it was pierced by the clang of a bell and the announcer's "That's the bell for round three, ladies and gentlemen."

As I pushed my way into the Store I wondered if the announcer gave any thought to the fact that he was addressing as "ladies and gentlemen" all the Negroes around the world who sat sweating and praying, glued to their "master's voice."

There were only a few calls for RC Colas, Dr. Peppers, and Hire's root beer. The real festivities would begin after the fight. Then even the old Christian ladies who taught their children and tried themselves to practice turning the other cheek would buy soft drinks, and if the Brown Bomber's victory was a particularly bloody one they would order peanut patties and Baby Ruths also.

Bailey and I lay the coins on top of the cash register. Uncle Willie didn't allow us to ring up sales during a fight. It was too noisy and might shake up the atmosphere. When the gong rang for the next round we pushed through the near-sacred quiet to the herd of children outside.

"He's got Louis against the ropes and now it's a left to the body and a right to the ribs. Another right to the body, it looks like it was low. . . . Yes, ladies and gentlemen, the referee is signaling, but the contender keeps raining the blows on Louis. It's another to the body, and it looks like Louis is going down."

My race groaned. It was our people falling. It was another lynching, yet another Black man hanging on a tree. One more woman ambushed and raped. A Black boy whipped and maimed. It was hounds on the trail of a man running through slimy swamps. It was a white woman slapping her maid for being forgetful.

The men in the Store stood away from the walls and at attention. Women greedily clutched the babes on their laps while on the porch the shufflings and smiles, flirtings and pinching of a few minutes before were gone. This might be the end of the world. If Joe lost we were back in slavery and beyond help. It would all be true, the accusations that we were lower types of human beings. Only a little higher than the apes. True that we were stupid and ugly and lazy and dirty and unlucky and, worst of all, that God Himself hated us and ordained us to be hewers of wood and drawers of water, forever and ever, world without end.

We didn't breathe. We didn't hope. We waited.

"He's off the ropes, ladies and gentlemen. He's moving towards the center of the ring." There was no time to be relieved. The worst might still happen.

"And now it looks like Joe is mad. He's caught Carnera with a left hook to the head and a right to the head. It's a left jab to the body and another left to the head. There's a left cross and a right to the head. The contender's right eye is bleeding and he can't seem to keep his block up. Louis is penetrating every block. The referee is moving in, but Louis sends a left to the body and it's the uppercut to the chin and the contender is dropping. He's on the canvas, ladies and gentlemen."

Babies slid to the floor as women stood up and men leaned toward the radio.

"Here's the referee. He's counting. One, two, three, four, five, six, seven . . . Is the contender trying to get up again?"

All the men in the Store shouted, "NO."

"—eight, nine, ten." There were a few sounds from the audience, but they seemed to be holding themselves in against tremendous pressure.

"The fight is all over, ladies and gentlemen. Let's get the microphone over to the referee. . . . Here he is. He's got the Brown Bomber's hand, he's holding it up. . . . Here he is. . . ."

Then the voice, husky and familiar, came to wash over us— "The winnah, and still heavyweight champeen of the world . . . Joe Louis."

Champion of the world. A Black boy. Some Black mother's son. He was the strongest man in the world. People drank Coca-Colas like ambrosia and ate candy bars like Christmas. Some of the men went behind the Store and poured white lightning in their soft-drink bottles, and a few of the bigger boys followed them. Those who were not chased away came back blowing their breath in front of themselves like proud smokers.

It would take an hour or more before the people would leave the Store and head for home. Those who lived too far had made arrangements to stay in town. It wouldn't do for a Black man and his family to be caught on a lonely country road on a night when Joe Louis had proved that we were the strongest people in the world.

A Second Look

1. Sometimes a writer deliberately exaggerates or overstates in order to make a point. Find several examples of such exaggeration in Angelou's narrative.

2. Why is Louis's victory so important to the listeners in the country store?

3. When we expect characters to behave in a certain way, but their behavior turns out to be the opposite of what we expect, that is one kind of irony. Explain the irony in paragraphs 13 and 28.

A Cyberlook

Many people feel that as a woman who has risen from a very humble background to achieve fame and success, a woman whose work is admired by both common readers and world leaders, Maya Angelou should herself be considered a hero. To learn more about her views (as well as those of a famous friend), see "Power Moves" (A Conversation with Maya Angelou and Eleanor Holmes Norton) on *InfoTrac College Edition*. Search the term "Maya Angelou." You can find other information about Angelou using any web browser.

Ideas for Writing

1. Choose one of the following statements:

"Even though they play for fame and money, professional athletes can be real heroes."

"Professional athletes are in sports for the fame and money; they should not be considered real heroes."

Use the statement you choose as the main idea in an essay. Support your opinion with examples of sports figures you feel are or are not heroic. Remember that you must make your idea of "hero" clear before you can show that professional athletes do or do not qualify. Assume that your readers have not yet made up their minds on this issue. You must convince them.

2. Write a paragraph or two in which you describe the tension and excitement of the crowd just before a sports event begins. The writing will be much easier if you have a specific event in mind and let the reader know what it is. Here is a sample topic sentence: "Just before the tip-off of the city basketball championship game, energy surged through the crowd like electricity."

Stride Toward Freedom

Martin Luther King, Jr.

Looking Forward

In these paragraphs, Martin Luther King, Jr., who was himself a hero and probably the greatest leader in the history of the American civil rights movement, describes a simple action that many people saw as an act of heroism—a black woman refusing to give up her seat to a white man on a bus in Montgomery, Alabama, at that time a highly segregated city. At the same time, Reverend King is explaining why something happened: this action marked the beginning of the famous Montgomery bus boycott. For days, the blacks of Montgomery refused to ride the public buses, leaving them nearly empty. This became a turning point in the civil rights movement, but its beginning was a single, brave act.

Help with Words

accommodate *(paragraph 1):* make room for
speculation *(paragraph 2):* an opinion formed without enough evidence
plausible *(paragraph 2):* believable
persistent *(paragraph 2):* occurring again and again
invariable *(paragraph 2):* unchanging
unwarranted *(paragraph 3):* without foundation, undeserved
intrepid *(paragraph 3):* fearless
affirmation *(paragraph 3):* a strong positive statement
accumulated *(paragraph 3):* piled up
indignities *(paragraph 3):* disgraces, humiliations
aspirations *(paragraph 3):* desires, ambitions
impeccable *(paragraph 4):* without fault

On December 1, 1955, an attractive Negro seamstress, Mrs. Rosa Parks, boarded the Cleveland Avenue bus in downtown Montgomery. She was returning home after her regular day's work in the Montgomery Fair—a leading department store. Tired from long hours on her feet, Mrs. Parks sat down in the first seat behind the section reserved for whites. Not long after she took her seat, the bus operator ordered her, along with three other Negro passengers, to move back in order to accommodate boarding white passengers. By this time every seat in the bus was taken. This meant that if Mrs. Parks followed the driver's command she would have to stand while a white male passenger, who had just boarded the bus, would sit. The other three Negro passengers immediately complied with the driver's request. But Mrs. Parks quietly refused. The result was her arrest.

There was to be much speculation about why Mrs. Parks did not obey the driver. Many people in the white community argued that she had been "planted" by the NAACP in order to lay the groundwork for a test case, and at first glance that explanation seemed plausible, since she was a former secretary of the local branch of the NAACP. So persistent and persuasive was this argument that it convinced many reporters from all over the country. Later on, when I was having press conferences three times a week—in order to accommodate the reporters and journalists who came to Montgomery from all over the world—the invariable first question was: "Did the NAACP start the bus boycott?"

But the accusation was totally unwarranted, as the testimony of both Mrs. Parks and the officials of the NAACP revealed. Actually, no one can understand the action of Mrs. Parks unless he realizes that eventually the cup of endurance runs over, and the human personality cries out, "I can take it no longer." Mrs. Parks's refusal to move back was her intrepid affirmation that she had had enough. It was an individual expression of a timeless longing for human dignity and freedom. She was not "planted" there by the NAACP, or any other organization; she was planted there by her personal sense of dignity and self-respect. She was anchored to that seat by the accumulated indignities of days gone by and the boundless aspirations of generations yet unborn. She was a victim of both the forces of history and the forces of destiny. She had been tracked down by the Zeitgeist—the spirit of the time.

Fortunately, Mrs. Parks was ideal for the role assigned to her by history. She was a charming person with a radiant personality, soft spoken and calm in all situations. Her character was impeccable and her dedication deep-rooted. All of these traits together made her one of the most respected people in the Negro community.

AFTERWORD

The Rosa and Raymond Parks Institute for Self-Development in Detroit is an organization that works primarily to improve the lives and self-images of children and young people. In a 1992 interview, one of the teenage girls with whom Rosa Parks had worked said: "Mrs. Parks doesn't think of herself as a heroine. She did it because it was right. She doesn't see herself as the Mother of the Civil Rights movement, but I see her as that. All children do."

So do many others. On 19 January 1999, Rosa Parks was one of the honored guests invited to sit with Mrs. Clinton when the President delivered his State of the Union Address. In recognizing Mrs. Parks, the President said: ". . . For most of us alive today, in a very real sense, this journey [toward racial unity and equality] began 43 years ago, when a woman named Rosa Parks sat down on a bus in Alabama, and wouldn't get up. She's sitting down with the First Lady tonight, and she may get up or not, as she chooses. We thank her." Later that same year Mrs. Parks received the Congressional Medal of Honor, the highest award given to a United States civilian.

A Second Look

1. King's essay (of which this is the beginning) shows cause and effect: Mrs. Parks's arrest was a cause; the bus boycott was the effect. He also shows cause–and–effect relationships in paragraphs 1 and 3. What are they?

2. Near the end of paragraph 3, King emphasizes the importance of his point by attracting our attention with repetition. Find several examples. Would even more repetition be effective? Why or why not?

3. In paragraph 1, King tells us a good deal about Mrs. Parks, mentioning her appearance, occupation, place of employment, and so forth. Since it is her action that becomes important, why does King give so much personal information about her? Is this a successful writing technique?

4. Moving from a bus seat may seem a small matter. Why did Mrs. Parks choose to go to jail rather than leave her seat?

5. In paragraph 3, King says that Mrs. Parks was "tracked down by . . . the spirit of the time." Why was the time right for an action such as hers?

A Cyberlook

1. Commenting on her 1955 action, Mrs. Parks has said: "I was there. I took that stand. I think the Lord gave me the strength and the courage to resist the way I was being treated." To read Mrs. Parks's thoughts on this and related topics, see the interview that was published in *Christianity Today*, 24 April 1995. It is available on *InfoTrac College Edition*. Search under "Rosa Parks."

2. In September, 1996, Mrs. Parks received the Presidential Medal of Freedom Award. To read President Clinton's remarks upon presenting the award (and to give yourself a modest Internet challenge), do the following: Access the *White House Electronic Publications* site. Scroll down to Search Documents by Words and Document Type. Enter the words "Rosa Parks." Set the Start Date at September 1, 1996 and the End Date at September 30, 1996. Then click on Search Documents. When the list comes up, click on President Remarks at Medal of Freedom Awards Ceremony. If you have difficulty finding the site, go to the *Wadsworth Developmental English* web page and click on Textbook Resource Centers.

Ideas for Writing

1. Sometimes a personal event such as Mrs. Parks's refusal to move or Joe Louis's fight can take on importance for large groups of people. The same is true for events involving relatively small numbers of people, such as the actions of freedom fighters currently struggling in a number of countries throughout the world. In small groups or as a class, discuss recent examples. You might include anything from an individual speaking out against unfair treatment to a student protest to an Olympic victory or a sports championship. The only condition is that the events you name must have taken on importance for a larger group beyond the individuals or small groups involved, making those persons heroic.

   Choose one of these events as the subject of an essay. When you write, first describe the event for readers who may not be familiar with it. Tell about the person or persons involved. Explain clearly what they did. Then go on to show your readers why this event was important to others and why those you are writing about are heroes.

2. Complete the following sentence: "I would rather go to jail than _____ ." Then write a paragraph (or even a whole essay) using this statement as the topic sentence or thesis and explaining why you feel so strongly about your subject.

Making Connections

Working in small groups, make of list of people whom you consider heroic. Consider the individuals described in the essays in this unit, as well as the names you may have collected in the *Cyberlook* assignment on page 166. After discussion, select the names to go on a Top Ten Modern Heroes list. Then write a definition of *hero* that will cover all the persons your group considers heroic.

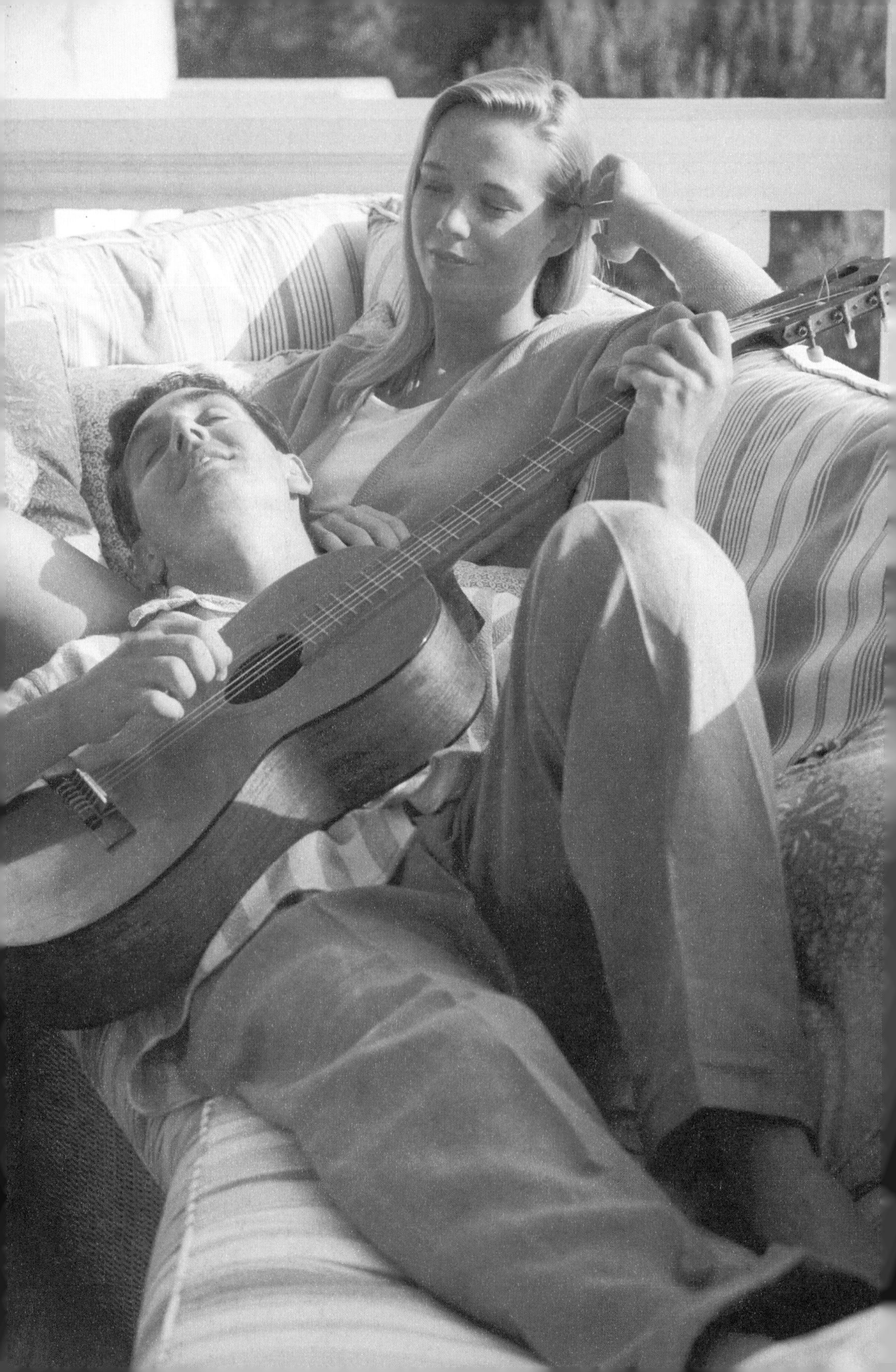

Women and Men

Women and men are, after all, just the female and male of the same species, yet they may sometimes appear to be unrelated beings or natural enemies. The first three writers in this unit find that women and men can successfully develop friendly or loving relationships, but it takes mutual effort and understanding. The final two writers focus on women's need to develop their potential in a world that often encourages them not to be their best.

Yes, Women and Men Can Be "Just Friends"

Marjorie Franco

Looking Forward

In this essay, Marjorie Franco begins with examples from her youth and builds up to the main idea, which is stated in paragraph 5. She shows by the arrangement of her ideas that men and women must first establish their own identities before they can form real friendships.

Help with Words

platonic *(paragraph 3):* free from sexual desire
mutual *(paragraph 4):* common or shared
astounded *(paragraph 4):* shocked or amazed
psychotherapist *(paragraph 5):* one who treats psychological disorders
siblings *(paragraph 5):* brothers and sisters
discomfiting *(paragraph 6):* causing discomfort

I remember a summer day when I was ten years old: I was walking my dog, Lucky, in the South Side Chicago neighborhood where I grew up. Lucky strained at his leash, sniffing the trunk of the neighborhood's favorite climbing tree. Suddenly a

183

wild shout startled me: "Look out, Rehn Peterson's sister!" and I saw Teddy Wilson, my brother's friend, on his Silver King bicycle, bearing down on me at top speed. With great presence of mind I leaped aside and, to Lucky's astonishment, slammed hard against the tree. I was furious—not because I'd been very nearly run down by a bike, and not because I'd had the wind knocked out of me by a tree. I was outraged because Teddy Wilson had denied me my identity.

On that day something stirred in me. Until then I had given little thought to who I was. My brother, two years older, was close to me; I was his friend and I knew it. He had other friends, of course, boys—they were always around—and because I was my brother's friend I had assumed I was their friend, too. But on that summer day, in the eyes of Teddy Wilson, I was "Rehn Peterson's sister" and nothing more.

But I wanted more. And in the years that followed, because of that drive for identity, I gained some practical experience in platonic friendship. Never mind that my girlfriend Florence, who read *True Story*, had whispered hotly into my ear, "Boys have uncontrollable passions, and they can't help it." I hadn't noticed any uncontrollable passion, unless you want to count the time Teddy Wilson said I looked fat in my bathing suit, and in that case the uncontrollable passion was mine.

I became friends with my brother's friends and remained so until we all grew up and scattered from the neighborhood. As a friend, I went with Roy to his senior prom because his girlfriend was out of town; I went to plays with Elmer because we had developed a mutual interest in the theater; I learned to cook with Jack since we both liked to cook (we experimented in our parents' kitchens and astounded each other with unusual creations). And eventually I went for long walks with Teddy Wilson during which we told each other our troubles.

My early experiences laid the groundwork for the attitudes I carried into adult life. In a recent discussion with David M. Moss, Ph.D., psychotherapist on the staff of Lutheran General Hospital's Consultation Center in Park Ridge, Illinois, he told me, "The development of healthy friendships grows out of the trust we learn and experience in childhood. Self-trust and trust of others are learned as early as the first year in life. From then on the presence or absence of trust is relearned and reexperienced in relationships with siblings, peers, and authority figures." I learned from my experience that it is not only possible but also desirable and highly rewarding for women and men to have platonic friendships. Shared interests between a man and woman need not include sex.

"The richness of platonic relationships can be enjoyed," says Dr. Moss, "if we draw responsible boundaries in our use of sexuality." However, choosing to have platonic friendships does not necessarily correspond to what may be in the minds of others. Pressures from outside a relationship can be very discomfiting.

Is it worth it, then? That depends. It's easier to be what others expect us to be. It would have been easy for me to remain Rehn Peterson's sister and let it go at that. Claiming identity is an effort. But the effort has given me the pleasures of friendship and good memories I will always keep.

A Second Look

1. According to the author, how is a strong self-identity related to platonic friendship?
2. It is possible to define a term without ever using a dictionary definition. What is Franco's method of defining platonic friendships in paragraph 5? It is also possible to define by giving examples. What examples of platonic friendships does the author mention?
3. Why does Franco begin the essay with a personal experience? Point out some of the specific details that make the description of the experience interesting.

A Cyberlook

Marjorie Franco's article was written in the mid-1970s. Have the opportunities for developing platonic friendships grown better with the passing years? Catherine Walsh looks at the possibilities of heterosexual friendships for "baby boomers and post-boomers" in "Perspectives," a column appearing in *America* (1997). You can read it on *InfoTrac College Edition*. Search the term "platonic friendships."

Ideas for Writing

1. Write about a relationship with someone you consider a platonic friend. Begin by choosing the person; then list the interests you have in common. Recall some specific experiences that show these common interests, and arrange them from earliest to most recent or from least to most important. When you write about this relationship, assume that your readers know what a platonic friendship is but that they have never met the friend you are describing.

2. Have you ever been treated like someone's son, daughter, brother, sister, or friend rather than as an individual? Describe that experience. Remember to use specific details.

Skiing with the Guys

Catherine Ettlinger

Looking Forward

When Catherine Ettlinger, former managing editor of *Mademoiselle* magazine, went heli-skiing with a group of advanced skiers, she found herself the only woman in the company of eleven men, "a macho bunch." In this article, she describes how she was able to become "one of the guys" and keep her feminine identity at the same time.

Help with Words

careened *(paragraph 1):* tilted
pangs *(paragraph 2):* pains
pervasive *(paragraph 4):* widespread
relishing *(paragraph 6):* greatly enjoying
tabloid *(paragraph 6):* a newspaper often featuring sensational stories and headlines
non sequitur *(paragraph 8):* something that does not follow logically
preamble *(paragraph 8):* introductory remarks
veritable *(paragraph 9):* actual
litany *(paragraph 16):* series
epiphany *(paragraph 17):* a sudden revelation
maliciously *(paragraph 17):* cruelly or viciously
prowess *(paragraph 18):* ability
precariously *(paragraph 23):* dangerously
precluded *(paragraph 24):* prevented
traverses *(paragraph 25):* cross-overs
rendered *(paragraph 28):* made
pariah *(paragraph 28):* a misfit or outcast

The helicopter careened, climbed, dove, floated and hovered until a safe landing was found: the point of a peak that dropped sharply on all four sides, a vertical view down a mountainside in the Canadian Rockies that fell into the sky.

We stayed close to put on our skis, and then, following our guide, Ian, one by one so as not to loosen the snow and start a slide, we edged around the shoulder of the peak until we came to the mouth of a wide gully that dropped at a 40-degree angle, one of the steepest pitches I'd ever seen. Just me and eleven guys, strangers in pursuit of the ultimate ski experience. And though I'd done this before (this was my third trip heli-skiing with Canadian Mountain Holidays in the boonies of British Columbia), can-I-keep-up pangs were now gathering in my gut.

Two of the guys started down after Ian, then two more, making tracks that slithered away like snakes in the thigh-high April powder. The six others looked to me. This would be my reckoning. I pushed off the lip, catching air (always good for points) and sank into the champagne powder. As I rose to make my first turn I had my rhythm: two, three, four turns, free-falling down the steep from one to another, face shot after face shot of powder dusting my glasses. After two dozen or so turns, the pitch flattened and my tight turns became lovely, long loopy ones. Easing from edge to edge and back again, I pulled up to the others, thinking this was the absolute best that skiing has to offer. Endless expanses of virgin wilderness in every direction. I felt like one of the luckiest people alive.

It wasn't easy being a girl among guys out for a pure jock experience. Pervasive in the lodge is a locker-room logic that turns avalanche scares and close-call falls into badges of courage—and any woman into a stereotype who associates powder more with makeup than skiing and who never goes anywhere her blow-dryer can't go.

It had taken me two days to get into this group. I was put at first with those who had come for the "Learn to Ski Powder Week"; no questions asked, it went without saying that I couldn't keep up with the big boys. But I was bored until I was moved up to the intermediate level in the afternoon. The next day I was promoted to the advanced group—a macho bunch—and skied with them until high winds forced us back to the lodge just before lunch the next day (the lodges are so isolated, they can be reached only by helicopter in the winter).

Deciding not to waste the afternoon indoors, I put on cross-country skis and took off along an old logging road, relishing the majesty of the mountains and the solitude. About an hour out I saw some cat tracks (as in cougar), and the city side of me did an about-face. I headed home to the lodge, visions of gruesome tabloid headlines dancing in my mind. Going along at a pretty good clip I ran into two guys heading out.

"Beautiful, isn't it?" I asked.

"Great exercise" was one guy's retort—a non sequitur, I thought. That night after dinner the same guy, Reb (yes, that's short for Rebel—he'd already won points for wearing a T-shirt and shell when everyone else was bundled up in down), sat next to me and, without any preamble, asked, "Why aren't you married?" I asked why he was, and left for the far side of the room.

I'd encountered the same sort of boldness on my second heli-ski trip: Early in the week three men, veritable strangers, had asked me to spend the night with them. At the time I was insulted. In retrospect, I realized the offers were merely an extension of the macho flexing that underscores the whole heli-ski experience—and puts me, as a woman, on the outside.

Imagine how I felt, then, when the next morning at breakfast Reb turned up again: "We had a deserter in our group; a guy was called back home for some emergency. Wanna join up?"

Like the army? "Is this a joke?" I asked. His was the fastest group of the four.

"Nope. We want a woman."

"Filling a quota?"

"No, seriously, we heard you're a real good skier, and we'd like it very much if you'd join us."

In that case (skier first, woman second): "Sure."

As my new group waited for the helicopter to pick us up in front of the lodge, Dave, a third-year law student, began a litany of the dirtiest dirty jokes I'd ever heard. Was this for my benefit, to make me feel uncomfortable? The sinking feeling in the pit of my stomach returned. After we landed the jokes started all over again. Then Howard, a friend of Reb's and one of his three ski buddies from California, stepped to the edge of the ledge to urinate. Ian, our guide that day (the four guides rotate from group to group), warned, "Howard, watch it, you're getting kind of close." We all looked over, worried. Ian added: "Howard, you don't have much to hang on to out there." I was the first to laugh. . . .

Suddenly everything was different: I was one of the guys. I could ski, and I could join in the fun too. Then and there I had an epiphany of sorts: Those dirty jokes weren't maliciously intended to make me feel uneasy and unwanted; they were simply part of the experience. Had they not told those jokes on my account, that would indeed have made me an outsider.

A funny thing happened after I joined the fraternity: My "prowess" allowed me to be treated like a "princess." Now whoever was the doorman (last in, first out of the helicopter) offered me a hand. Whoever was the tail and carried the reserve pack always asked if I wanted him to carry anything extra. Whoever saw my skis unloaded before I did would hand them to me. I felt protected. In return I was expected to ski hard. Run after run, as we held up our ends of the unspoken bargain, I began to see heli-skiing as the essence of the whole man/woman thing: Men being their most boyish like to treat women (who can cut it) like girls.

That first night I joined the group I took extra care dressing for dinner. These guys knew I could ski and laugh at their dirty jokes . . . now it was time to identify myself as pure woman. I purposefully picked my pink shirt (prettier) over the blue one with stars (funkier); leggings (sexier) over jeans (jockier). And I chose black flats, no socks over just socks (sloppy) or sneakers (clunky). My hair, which one guy told me he loved because it was so natural (it was a mess! I'll never understand men!), got moussed and sprayed and scrunched until it was unnaturally full and curly; then I tied on a bow and, from my earlobes, hung pink gemstone hearts that matched my shirt. The result: Coco Chanel Goes Skiing.

The group saved me a seat (dinner is family style), and over good food and wine I heard about money-making innovations and miserable marriages, management techniques and dual-career controversies, new restaurants and new reads. By dessert we'd crossed an emotional line equal to the physical one we'd crossed that day—and created a bond. Little did I know, it would be put to the test the next morning.

The daily rotation had given us the first-group spot. . . . The company photographer, up for the week to shoot pictures for the new brochure, wanted to join our group because 1) we could make perfect turns and 2) we were first out and would take the first untracked lines down the glacier we were headed for. The problem was that our group had no space, so if he were to join, someone would have to drop back to a less skillful group. I realized that I, having no seniority, would be the "guy" to go.

Instead, a couple of the guys went to the guide room and said, "We've got a great group, no laggers, and we want to keep it intact." No names, nothing. That was that.

The sky broke blue that morning, and the first run out we landed in the crease between two peaks on Conrad Glacier. We skied the wide-open glacier most of the morning, then we chopper-hopped over to a run called Scapula for some skiing through trees. "OK, now we'll see if you can ski the tough stuff." With that, Thierry, our guide that day, started down. We followed him around patches of pines until we reached a precariously steep mountainside hugged by trees so huge they left little ski space between them. "Get partners and stick together," he said. "I'll go down and make the left border; over there several hundred meters is a drop—that's your right border. I'll wait at the bottom." And he was off, yodeling so we could hear the right direction.

Just before I felt like the uncoordinated, unpopular third-grade kid who's always last picked for the team, Reb, the best of the bunch, picked me. (Skier's etiquette precluded me from choosing him, because he's better than I and I would slow his run.) "I'll follow you," he said. Okay. Go for it.

I took a breath and shoved off. Fast. Hard. Straight down, no traverses. Feel it. Don't think it. Tight. One turn after another, and another. Breathe. Ducking, dodging branches. In the air. Turn again, again, again. Breathe. Faster. He's on my tail. Go, give it all you've got. Now. More. Keep it up. Another turn and another. And then I fell, skis skewed to avoid tumbling into a tree well. He fell too but only to avoid crashing into me. Practically gasping for air, I looked over, a "sorry" on my face. Smiling, he said, "Thanks, that was the best of the week."

Though I knew he'd have made the whole run (and knew he knew it too) if he'd gone with someone else, he meant what he said. It was a great run, maybe not as fast and furious as it might have been, but it was great in another sense: He'd pushed me, I was able to meet the challenge respectably, and he relished that—and seemed to take (more than) equal credit for my performance. It was as though he'd given birth to the skier in me.

27   The harder I skied the better I got, and I felt the others too took pleasure in my progress. Like when Dave coaxed me over a (huge!) jump and I made it. Like when Buck, one of the guides, insisted I carry the reserve pack, knowing I could . . . and I could. Like when Howard said to follow right behind him, no stopping, top to bottom, and I did. Like when I skied too far below the cutoff to the helicopter landing and had to climb up a couple hundred feet in a thigh-deep powder and I did it, and the next runs too, never holding anyone up.

28   And they took equal pleasure in the idea that I was female, that I would wear a pink bow in my hair and hearts in my ears. What had first rendered me a pariah, the notion that I was a city woman whose idea of enjoying the outdoors was to open my window, finally tipped the scale to achieve in the most perfect wilderness a perfect balance between the sexes.

A Second Look

1. Ettlinger begins with a description of a particular skiing experience. When do you begin to see what her true subject will be? Should she have indicated it earlier? Why or why not?

2. One way in which Ettlinger shows, rather than tells, her readers what happens is by using lively verbs and accurate, interesting adjectives. Pick out several examples.

3. The writer uses at least two levels of language in this essay: fairly formal and very informal. Pick out examples of both. Why do you think she mixes these levels? Do you feel that this technique is effective? Why or why not?

4. How does Ettlinger attack the locker-room prejudice of the other skiers?

5. Ettlinger says she became "one of the guys" while keeping her identity "as pure woman." Do you agree, or do you think she went against her own standards of feminine behavior? Explain.

A Cyberlook

More than some other sports, skiing long remained a male domain. Yet in 1957, the first woman joined the U.S. Snow Rangers. Her name was Jerry Colburn Nunn, and her application to the Rangers was accepted only because her name led officials to think she was a man. Against great odds, she had a successful career. You can read her story in "Hall of Fame: Jerry Colburn Nunn—For Breaking into an Old Boy's Club" published in *Skiing* magazine (December, 1997). Go to *InfoTrac College Edition* and search under "women's skiing."

Ideas for Writing

1. Reread paragraphs 3 and 25. Notice how Ettlinger describes action. Try writing a paragraph or two of your own describing a short period of rapid, intense action such as that of skiing, skating, running, or gymnastics.

2. Tell of an experience in which you were accepted by a group that formerly had excluded you. Tell your readers exactly what the group was, why it excluded you, and what you did to gain acceptance into it.

3. Marjorie Franco and Catherine Ettlinger both write about platonic friendships, but they differ in their description of how these friendships are formed. In a paragraph or two, summarize the differences in their points of view. If your instructor wishes, you may work on this assignment in small groups.

Significant Other

Rick Weiss

Looking Forward

Rick Weiss, a writer living in New York City, is married to Natalie Angier, science reporter for *The New York Times*. In this essay, Weiss describes how he and his wife-to-be began competing even before they met, how they made accommodations for their two careers, and how he came to accept a role that at first seemed very strange to him.

Help with Words

harried *(paragraph 3):* disturbed, under stress
cachet *(paragraph 4):* distinction, mark of quality
prestigious *(paragraph 5):* distinguished, impressive
relinquishment *(paragraph 6):* yielding, giving up something
precluded *(paragraph 6):* prevented
anarchist *(paragraph 8):* radical, revolutionary
indoctrinated *(paragraph 8):* taught, trained
accolades *(paragraph 10):* honors, tributes
mantles *(paragraph 10):* cloaks or coverings; here, used as a figure of speech
accouterment *(paragraph 11):* pieces of equipment, accessory
penumbral *(paragraph 11):* shadowy
placid *(paragraph 12):* calm
vapid *(paragraph 12):* dull, without imagination
unabridged *(paragraph 16):* complete
aspiration *(paragraph 16):* ambition, desire

My wife and I will probably never agree on the way I introduced myself on that spring day, during a coffee break at a National Institutes of Health conference.

In my memory it was friendly, something like, "Hey, congratulations on getting the job at *The Times.*" But she remembers the greeting as less than cordial: "Hi, I'm Rick Weiss. You got my job."

Moreover, she claims (and she may be right about this) that I added, "And from the look of how harried you are, I'm not really jealous."

The fact is, she was a bit of a wreck. It was her first month on the job—a much sought after science-writing position for which I and others had competed. That day the story was big, her deadline was approaching, and she couldn't find a phone jack for her laptop's modem. In contrast, I was working for a weekly magazine and wasn't under pressure; my deadline was four days away. But my relaxed pace came with a price. No matter how well written, my article would never carry the cachet of hers. And her paycheck, I supposed, would make mine look like a drugstore coupon.

Whether or not I let slip a touch of envy, our introduction marked the start of some serious soul-searching on my part. The bottom line is, I'm one of those guys whose wife has the more prestigious job. She's a big-time journalist, writing stories I wanted to write myself.

What's more, my falling in love with this hotshot competitor was only the beginning of a slippery slope of professional and personal relinquishment. Because she lived in New York and I in Washington, we became weekend regulars on the Metroliner. But an allergy to the mildew in my swampy basement quickly precluded her from visiting, and it was I who had to elbow my way through Friday evening crowds at Union Station and, worse, stumble through Penn Station every Monday morning at six for the train back to Washington.

When it became clear we'd have to rearrange our lives to accommodate our love, it was I who gave up my job and relocated to Manhattan, where a depressed publishing market forced me to take a corporate job that left me in journalistic obscurity.

So what's the big deal? After all, I grew up in the 60s and spent my formative years in California in a twenty-five member anarchist commune that left me well indoctrinated in feminist principles. In those days, even armed revolution seemed an appropriate means of securing for working women their proper place in the power structure.

Besides, I'm basically a self-assured person with a good sense of humor. So I've been able to shrug a lot of this off with what's become a standard joke: "She's got the job, but I've got her."

But it's not that simple. As the only boy in a Jewish family, I grew up believing I'd inherited a virtual guarantee of special standing. And as an adult things have pretty much gone my way, never forcing me to put my politically correct training to the test. So sure, I got the girl, but it seemed unfair that she got me and everything else—prestige, money, and public accolades. It's as though her snagging that job was the first of several lessons the universe figured I was owed—lessons about letting go of traditional mantles of power and discovering new and subtle sources of security as a man.

Now, when attending dinners related to my wife's work, I find myself more quiet than before, wondering whether I'm seen by others as a mere accouterment to my better-known partner. I find myself sympathizing with women at our table who I might previously have written off as "wives." I see that they, like me, have talents and accomplishments of their own—a truth I was not totally blind to before, but one that I couldn't fully appreciate until I entered the penumbral world of "the spouse."

Sometimes, out of defensiveness, I make the problem worse. Rather than offer clues about my skills and interests, I perform a silent experiment in sexual role reversal, in which I patiently wait to see whether anyone will bother asking me what I do or what I think. And again I discover new sympathy for my placid female counterparts, whose quiet smiles, I realize, may be more righteous than vapid.

But my newfound empathy for the mates of public figures is only part of the lesson of my current station in life. The bigger challenge has been to see through society's traditional emblems of power—fame and fortune—and abandon them for a more profound sense of self-confidence and self-worth.

At first I found solace in predictable harbors. At home I took heart in my ability to repair light switches, install shelves, and fix the shower faucet, while maintaining firm control over anything having to do with lawyers or accountants. And to retain the respect of fellow writers, I made a point of writing freelance articles for respected publications.

But over time it has become clear that power substitutes are only substitutes. With an appliance repaired here, an article published there, the contest would have been endless and I'd have found no peace.

So lately I've been experimenting with a new approach, embracing the unabridged, wretched, and remarkable truth of who I am, and also who I am not—what Zorba called "the whole catastrophe." That angle isn't new, of course. But it's difficult to really let go of power until you feel the deep fatigue that comes with trying to hold onto it—and until you accept the notion that an aspiration to excellence need not be a contest with winners and losers.

Recently I had the opportunity to test whether I had made any progress along these lines, when my wife was awarded a Pulitzer Prize for her writing at *The Times*. My heart flip-flopped when she called with the news; yes, there was a pang of jealousy, but most of all I was overjoyed about the recognition that she so clearly had earned.

Hailing a cab to go crosstown for a glass of champagne, I took pleasure in my heart's ratio of pride and envy. And recognizing, too, that I had not transcended competitiveness altogether, I braced myself for the speeches I knew her editors would give, congratulating themselves for the good judgment they showed in choosing to hire her.

A Second Look

1. What changes did Weiss make "to accommodate our love?"

2. Weiss states that he was "well indoctrinated in feminist principles." Why, then, did he find it hard to accept that his wife had a more prestigious job and a larger salary than he did? How does he finally come to terms with this problem?

3. At the time he is writing, is his adjustment to this situation complete? How do we know?

4. Where would you place Weiss's essay on a scale running from very informal to very formal. Explain your answer.

5. What kind of reading audiences do you think Weiss is writing for? Why do you think so?

A Cyberlook

1. Dual-employment relationships have caused shifting in traditional roles. When both partners hold jobs, who does the dishes? Who cleans the house? Does racial or ethnic background affect the division of labor? For a study of such questions, see Yoshinori Kamo and Ellen L. Cohen, "Division of Household Work Between Partners: A Comparison of Black and White Couples" in *Journal of Comparative Family Studies* (Spring, 1998). You will find this article on *InfoTrac College Edition*; search Powertrac under the author's names. Because this is a scholarly article, filled with rather technical language and data, you may want to scroll through until you come to the section entitled "Discussion and Conclusions."

2. There are literally thousands of Internet sites with information on gender roles; the quality ranges from excellent to useless. For a sampling, search "gender roles" using any search engine. (A tip: AltaVista is particularly useful for this kind of search.) Compare your results with those of your classmates. Do some issues seem to attract more interest and attention than others? Do you agree that these issues are important, or do you think interest in them will fade within a few years? Why? If your instructor wishes, small groups may prepare oral or written reports on Internet findings and your discussion of them.

Ideas for Writing

1. In one paragraph, summarize Weiss's attitude toward traditional gender roles at the time he met his wife-to-be.

2. Describe an experience in which you felt that you did not truly belong with a group but were there as just a wife, husband, brother, sister, or friend. Explain to your readers what the situation was, how you felt, and how you tried to cope or make yourself more comfortable.

3. Weiss writes that he is modern in his thinking, "indoctrinated in feminist principles," and self-assured. Yet for a time he finds it difficult to accept his own and his wife's personal and professional positions. Describe a situation in your own life when a firmly held belief has been challenged by a personal situation.

Keeping the Light On

Leonard Pitts, Jr.

Looking Forward

Newspaper columnist Leonard Pitts Jr. observes his daughter—a bright, high achieving, computer literate seven-year-old—and worries about early adolescence, a time "when it's no longer easy for girls to be smart." He tries to prepare her, but he knows the difficulty of keeping the intellectual light on.

Help with Words

validation *(paragraph 6)*: approval, declaration of worth
defer *(paragraph 6)*: to submit to the wishes or opinion of someone else
luminescent *(paragraph 11)*: glowing, shining with light
superficial *(paragraph 14)*: on the surface, shallow, unimportant
extracted *(paragraph 14)*: pulled out, removed with some force
tensile strength *(paragraph 17)*: resistance of a material to tearing or breaking when stretched and pulled (similar to elasticity)
deferential *(paragraph 18)*: courteous and respectful, especially to someone in a superior position; submissive (related to *defer*, paragraph 6)

My daughter is trying to cross a river of goo. 1

That is, she's on the computer next to me, playing 2
a game that's designed to enhance her educational skills. Crossing

the river, for instance, will require her to work out a numbers problem.

Middle of the summer and her brothers are whiling away the days watching television and playing basketball. But my little girl—my straight-A 7-year-old—is likely as not to be found here in my office, glued to the computer, learning.

Pardon me while I swell with pride.

After which, I'll cringe with fear.

If you've ever raised a girl, you might understand. If not, just know that there comes an age—early adolescence, usually—when it's no longer easy for girls to be smart. An age when knowing the answers and participating in class become almost acts of defiance. When the validation of boys becomes crucial and a girl learns that she must defer to male ego and vanity or else become an outcast.

I don't know how that feels, but I can tell you how it looks, because I've seen it.

It looks like a light going out.

And my daughter is filled with light.

Still skips from one destination to another. Still thinks "girls rule, boys drool," just about the coolest rhyme ever. Most of all, still sees no reason why she can't be just as smart as—or smarter than—some boy.

She is still luminescent as the sun.

And I, having seen too many girls go dark with the need to look good and seem simple, having seen too many women still sit dully in the shadows cast by men, buzz around her with but one mission in mind: To protect the light.

That's why I avoid spending a lot of time telling her how pretty she is. Not that she isn't the cutest little thing you ever saw, but I try instead to praise her for her ability to figure out a problem; I want her to value that more than she does her looks.

I've warned her that there's going to come a time when people will want to judge her solely on that superficial aspect. A time when being smart won't be as easy as it is now. And, silly as it sounds, I've extracted from her a promise against that day: "The first time somebody tells you that you can't be smart because you're a girl, tell them too bad. Tough. Deal with it."

A few months ago, I was talking with a dad I met in Atlanta about his girls. Phil's worried about his 15-year-old daughter, he said, because she's so focused on "trying to keep this reputation as this cool girl who older guys will call."

Phil's oldest girl, 17-years-old, doesn't trouble him as much. He says she tends to be tough, "and I like that, because I know she can handle the aggression of boys."

And it seems, on first blush, a heck of a thing to have to wish upon a girl, this toughness, this tensile strength. But the truth is, a girl coming of age at the millennium had better have some toughness in her, because the world she's going to enter certainly does. That world is hell on wimps and weaklings, sweeps away flowers and wisps.

Worse, it sends girls signals that often conflict and always confuse. Be deferential. Be aggressive. Be smart. Be simple. Be thin. Be big-chested. Be sweet. Be tough. Be a flirt. Be a lady.

Never, just be yourself. That's what a girl should hear. That should be enough. But it never is. Even women as accomplished as Barbara Walters and Janet Reno still struggle against double standards, restrictive perceptions, and confining expectations.

So I wonder what waits for my daughter in the years ahead. I watch her cross a river of goo and ask myself what she'll find on the other side.

She's a little girl filled with radiance. And I'm just struggling to hold back the dark.

A Second Look

1. Leonard Pitts's style is unusual. His essay violates several important guidelines for academic writing. For example, it is filled with one-sentence paragraphs and sentence fragments. Why do you think Pitts chooses to write this way? Is his style effective? Why or why not?

2. Pitts uses the word *light* several times. What does the light represent? What other words reinforce the imagery of light?

3. Why do many adolescent girls find it hard to be smart? What advice on this subject does Pitts give his daughter?

A Cyberlook

1. Leonard Pitts is a regular columnist for *The Miami Herald* and has twice won the National Headliner Award for his writing. To read more of his work, go to the *Miami Herald* web site. In the left-hand column under Sections, click on Voices. When that page loads, click on Leonard Pitts's image or name. If you have difficulty finding the site, go to the *Wadsworth Developmental English* web page and click on Textbook Resource Centers.

2. Ann Pollina, a teacher in an all-girls high school, argues that many efforts to improve girls' education in math, science, and technology have failed "because they have been aimed at making women think and behave like men." Noting recent research on the relation of gender to learning styles, Pollina gives specific suggestions for helping women succeed in male-dominated areas of study. You can read her article, "Gender Balance: Lessons from Girls in Science and Mathematics," on *InfoTrac College Edition*. Search the term "education of women," subdivision "technique."

Ideas for Writing

Based on your own experiences, the experiences of friends, and (if you wish) library or Internet searches, write an essay on one of the following topics:

1. Do schools and teachers, as well as peer pressure and society's expectations, encourage adolescent girls to hide their intellectual curiosity and ability (especially in math and science) in order to be popular and fit in?

2. Do schools and teachers, as well as peer pressure and society's expectations, encourage adolescent boys to hide their sensitivity and creativity (especially in literature and the arts) in order to be popular and fit in?

If your instructor wishes, small groups or the entire class may engage in discussion of these topics and share the preliminary planning for writing the essays.

Women Wasted

Jennifer Bitner

Looking Forward

In this student essay, Jennifer Bitner considers the differences among three generations of women. As she looks at her grandmother, her mother, and herself, she wonders whether the two older women ever felt as she does now.

Help with Words

aspirations *(paragraph 4):* wishes, ambitions
immersed *(paragraph 5):* totally involved

She sits in the living room of my aunt's house surrounded by blurry colors and shapeless movements. Noises come to her through layers of cotton. Ninety-five years have made her crumple and sag. She is a dying old creature.

She seems so happy; she smiles and hugs me to her softly. Her glassy eyes search out the blur that is my face and kiss it, missing my mouth, but giving me a wonderful nose kiss. In a way, her warm presence is comforting to me, but it also frightens me.

What is there to connect me to this strange old woman who lives strongly in the past, while I am searching for a future? What could I possibly share with someone so old, so near death? Was there any fun, any joy, in her life spent serving husband and children? When I look at an old picture of my grandmother, strange feelings come over me. I have a beautiful picture showing her at about my age. Her hair is pulled back in a soft bun, and her eyes are warm and proud. Her mouth is curved in my smile. I look like the woman in the picture, yet she is so far from the dying woman in the E-Z Boy rocker, and both are far from me.

If I could talk to the girl in the picture, would she be like me? Did she have many dreams? I am sure she dreamed of more than this. She must have had aspirations beyond motherhood, though she probably was not nearly as ambitious as I am. She was a woman at a time when woman meant wife and mother.

Fear hits me, the same fear I feel when I watch my mother clean the house or make my father's dinner. She is so immersed in these simple tasks, as if in a trance. I love these women, but my body and mind cry out that I will not be like them. I cannot confine myself to mindless tasks and unending service.

These women missed so much playing the role of wife and mother. Neither went to college; both stayed home and cared for children and house. They do not know what they missed out on—do they?

Does my mother ever get a vague feeling of distress? At night does she think, "Who am I and what have I done for myself? Where was my life in this tangle of years?"

Grandmother is too old to cry for. She smiles and in her semisenility is content, but I cry for my mother. The only job she ever held was as a secretary. Her life was spent in marriage and raising children. I know she gets depressed sometimes. Does she realize she has a mind she is wasting?

I cry for my mother, and her mother, and for all of the women who have been wasted. Minds, wonderful minds, wasted on dishes and hours of boredom. All of these things I think as I hug this old woman and hear the chatter of my mother in the next room gossiping.

A Second Look

1. One of the writer's strengths is her ability to give us clear pictures of people in just a few sentences. What details help us see what kind of women her grandmother and her mother are?

2. In paragraphs 2 and 5, Bitner says she feels fear. What is she afraid of? Why doesn't she express her fear more directly?

3. What is the writer's attitude toward the traditional role of women? What details indicate this attitude? Do you agree or disagree with her? Why?

Ideas for Writing

1. Perhaps you disagree with Jennifer Bitner's view of the role of wife and mother. (Review your answer to *A Second Look*, question 3.) If so, write a paper in which you give the advantages of a woman's remaining in the home to care for her family. You may wish to list both negative and positive aspects, but your main idea will be that there are still good reasons for a woman to choose the traditional role of wife and mother. If your instructor wishes, you could first discuss the topic in small groups.

2. If you are a woman reading this essay, you may feel as Bitner does when you compare yourself to your mother, aunts, grandmothers, or other older women in your family. If so, write a paper in which you describe their attitudes and yours, explaining the differences between them. You might consider Bitner's question: "They do not know what they missed out on—do they?"

3. If you are a man reading this essay, you may be able to look at your father and grandfather or other older men in your family and view the situation from their side. Do men of earlier generations have regrets—too much time spent at work and not enough at home, too many years when their children grew up almost without their noticing, too little time spent with their wives? If you think your life will be different, describe what those differences will be. In other words, write about Jennifer Bitner's topic from a male point of view.

Making Connections

Marjorie Franco writes that one difficulty in forming relationships is pressure from outside. This is true whether the relationships are personal or professional: in forming affiliations, we are often influenced by what others think. As Franco puts it: "It's easier to be what others expect us to be." In the selections in this unit, some of the women conform to what others expect of them, and some do not. Which women belong in which category? Considering what happens to these women, do you agree that "it's easier to be what others expect us to be?" And how does the pressure to "be what others expect us to be" affect young girls who are trying to develop their own self-images? Is the situation different for men and boys?

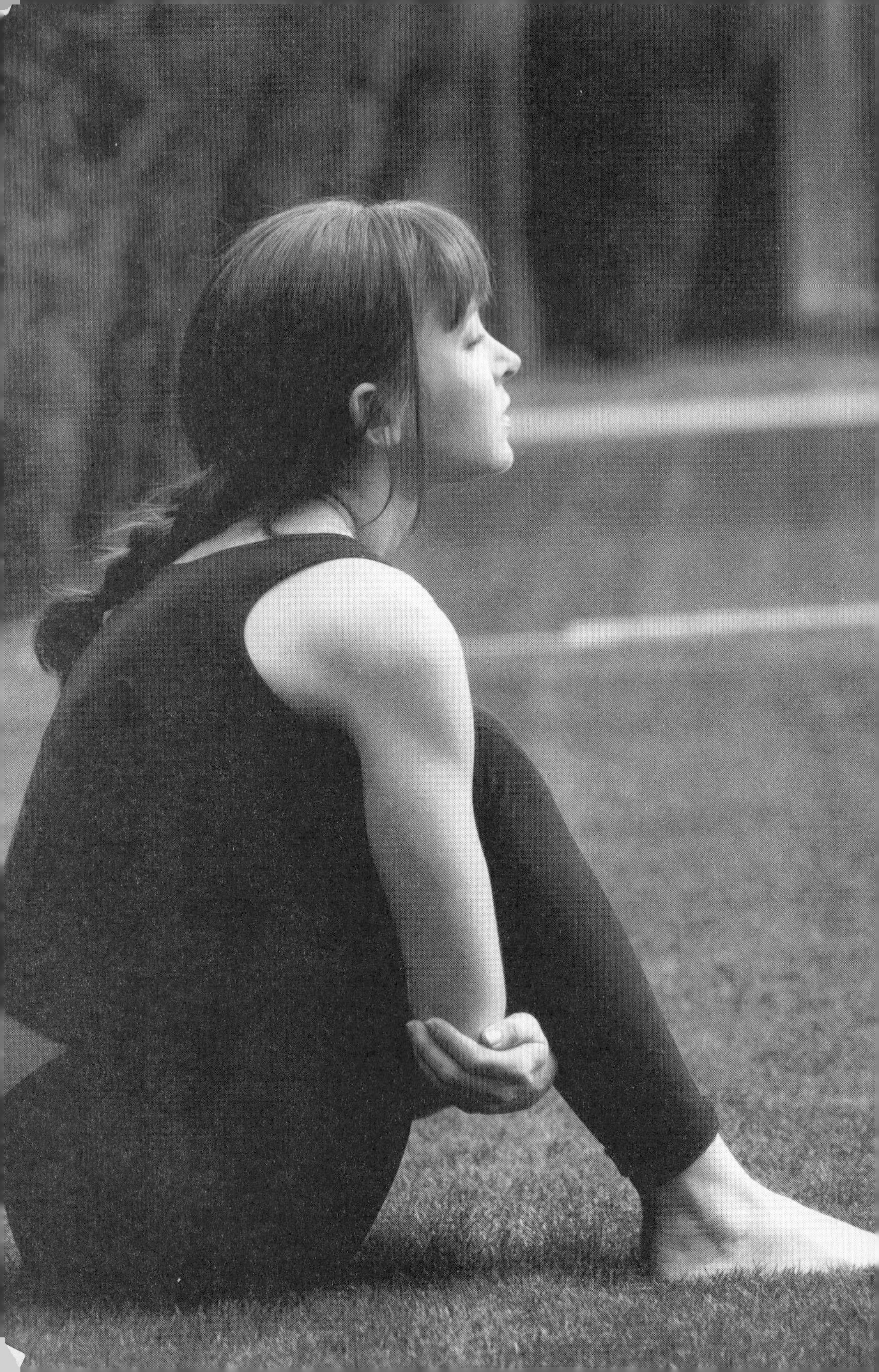

Health

Health—we think about it, talk about it, write about it, spend millions of dollars to achieve and maintain it, yet we can also find nearly countless ways to damage or destroy it. The essays in this unit look at four of the major health concerns of our time: eating disorders, AIDS, alcohol abuse, and smoking. The four writers have personal knowledge of their subjects, having suffered the effects of health problems themselves or watched with concern and sadness while others close to them did. Their narratives do not make happy reading, but they will make us think seriously about health issues and our obligations to ourselves and others.

Wasted

Marya Hornbacher

Looking Forward

Marya Hornbacher was twenty-three when she wrote *Wasted;* eating disorders had plagued her most of her life. Bulimia, a condition characterized by alternate binging and purging, began at age nine. Anorexia, which in its most extreme form can cause the victim literally to starve herself to death, set in at fifteen. When the condition reached its most severe level, Hornbacher, then in her early twenties, weighed only fifty-two pounds. Now, after medical treatment and counseling, the author is recovering; she does not believe she will ever be "cured." As you read, pay particular attention to the details that make the narrative so effective.

Help with Words

ascetic *(paragraph 1):* strict, plain and severe, lacking pleasure
hedonistic *(paragraph 1):* characterized by the love of pleasure and enjoyment
acclaimed *(paragraph 1):* praised, noted for
masochistic *(paragraph 2):* characterized by the desire to experience pain
appendage *(paragraph 4):* literally, something attached or appended; usually signifies some attachment or growth that is unwanted or considered useless
kamikaze *(paragraph 5):* a mission in which the agent is certain to die; a suicidal attack
precipitates *(paragraph 7):* causes something to happen quickly
mania *(paragraph 7):* an obsession or fixation
grandiose *(paragraph 10):* showy, overdone, unrealistically grand
blatantly *(paragraph 11):* glaringly, openly
raucous *(paragraph 13):* loud, shrill, noisy

I distinctly did not want to be seen as bulimic. I wanted to be an anorectic. I was on a mission to be another sort of person, a person whose passions were ascetic rather than hedonistic, who would Make It, whose drive and ambition were focused and pure, whose body came second, always, to her mind and her "art." I had no patience for my body. I wanted it to go away so that I could be a pure mind, a walking brain, admired and acclaimed for my incredible self-control. Bulimia simply did not fit into my image of what I would become. Still, I *was* bulimic and had been for seven years. It is no easy addiction to overcome. But my focus had changed.

Up to that point, the bulimia had had a life of its own. It was purely an emotional response to the world—under pressure, binge and purge; sad and lonely, binge and purge; feeling hungry, binge and purge—and actually had little to do, believe it or not, with a desire to lose weight. I'd always wanted to be thinner, sure, but I wanted to eat as well. The year I got to boarding school, I actually began to hate my body with such incredible force that my love of food was forced underground, my masochistic side surfaced, and anorexia became my goal.

Part of this had to do with the self-perpetuating nature of eating disorders: The worries about your weight do not decrease no matter how much weight you lose. Rather, they grow. And the more you worry about your weight, the more you are willing to act on that worry. You really do have to have an excessive level of body loathing to rationally convince yourself that starvation is a reasonable means to achieve thinness. Normally, there is a self-protective mechanism in the psyche that will dissuade the brain from truly dangerous activity, regardless of how desirable the effects of that activity may be. For example, a woman may wish to lose weight but have an essential respect for her physical self and therefore refrain from unhealthy eating. I had no such self-protective mechanism, no such essential self-respect. When you have no sense of physical integrity—a sense that your own health is important, that your body, regardless of shape, is something that requires care and feeding and a basic respect for the biological organism that it is—a very simple, all-too-common, truly frightening thing happens: You cross over from a vague wish to be thinner into a no-holds-barred attack on your flesh.

You stop seeing your body as your own, as something valuable, something that totes you around and does your thinking and feeling for you and requires an input of energy for this favor. You begin seeing it instead as an undesirable appendage, a wart you need to remove . . .

When you believe that *you* are not worthwhile in and of yourself, in the back of your mind you also begin to believe that *life* is not worthwhile in and of itself. It is only worthwhile insofar as it relates to your crusade. It is a kamikaze mission. Life and self are far less important than your single-minded goal. "Thinness" was as good a name as any for my goal. Twenty pounds, I said. No matter what.

By winter, I was starving. Malnutrition is not a joke. Whether you're skinny or not, your body is starving. As the temperature dropped, I began to grow fur, what is technically called lanugo. Your body grows it when you're not taking in enough calories to create internal heat (it's interesting how we think of calories as the Antichrist, rather than as an energy source). I liked my fur. I felt like a small bear. I grew fur on my belly, my ribs, the small of my back, my cheeks, fine downy fur, pale white. My skin grew whiter, more so than usual, when the sun became translucent, as it does in winter far north. I began to look a bit haunted. I stood in the shower, feeling the bones in my lower back, two small points at the top of my rear. I took hold of my pelvic bones, twin toy hatchets. I took Fiberall and Dexatrim. I drank gallons of water. I was perpetually cold.

Mornings, I'd haul myself out of bed at 5:00 a.m., put on running clothes, walk through the purple light latticed with the black arms of trees, open the doors to the long hall of the main building, and run. This was the strangest thing. I have always hated solitary exercise. When I was younger, I played soccer, racquetball, and swam on the swim team, but I had always, always hated solo running. I was very proud of myself for forcing my body to run. And run. Malnutrition precipitates mania. So does speed. Both were at play here, in large doses. But so was masochism—the subjection of the self and/or body to pain and fear, ultimately resulting in a transitory sense of mastery over pain and fear. Every morning, I ran five miles, up and down this hall, touching the door at each end, the mark of an obsession. I had to touch the door or else it didn't count. You make up these rules, and if you break the rules, God help you, you have to run an extra mile to make up for it. When I was done, I'd go downstairs to the workout room and weigh myself . . .

The workout room was packed with girls. On the scale, on the bikes, on the weights, the rowing machine. Nothing wrong with a little exercise. But in such a small community, you can't help but notice the changes. The same girls, shrinking, day after day. I saw them, later, on campus, shivering in classrooms, at readings, at concerts, wrapped in wool. I'd weigh myself and leave. There was no mutual recognition. You can talk food all day with friends, but you keep your secrets. On the surface, you're doing this companionably, you're a friggin' unstoppable dieting army and you'll all go down together. On the underside, you're all competing with one another to be the thinnest, most controlled, least weak, and you have your own private crusade on which no one can join you. . . .

By midwinter, I would run in the morning, eat grapefruit after grapefruit for breakfast (someone told me it had only eight calories. When I found out that was wrong, I ran ten miles to make up for all that grapefruit), go to class. At lunch I would speed-walk up and down the hallway while reading a book, then go to class. At the end of the day, run again, five more miles, go to the cafeteria, eat carrot sticks with mustard. Soon I made a new rule: now I had to run *after* dinner as well. By January I was running twenty-five miles a day, on a knee that was beginning to split.

In the hospitals, anorectics are always amazed that they could possibly have had the energy to run, to sit on the exercise bike for hours, pedaling madly toward the vanishing point in their heads. They talk about this in group, depending on their state of mind, with either a sad sort of pride, or shock. The latter is rare. You only hear the latter from women who have come to some understanding that they have been living in an altered state, a state that cannot be maintained. The former tend to maintain their grandiose illusion that they are superhuman.

I was beginning to harbor that delusion myself, that I was superhuman. When you coast without eating for a significant amount of time, and you are still alive, you begin to scoff at those fools who believe they must eat to live. It seems blatantly obvious to you that this is not true. You get up in the morning, you do your work, you run, you do not eat, you live.

You begin to forget what it means to live. You forget things. You forget that you used to feel all right. You forget what it means to feel all right because you feel like shit all of the time, and you can't remember what it was like before. People take the feeling of *full* for granted. They take for granted the feeling of steadiness, of hands that do not shake, heads that do not ache, throats not raw with bile and small rips from fingernails forced in haste to the gag spot. Stomachs that do not begin to dissolve with a battery-acid mixture of caffeine and pills. They do not wake up in the night, calves and thighs knotting with muscles that are beginning to eat away at themselves. They may or may not be awakened in the night by their own inexplicable sobs.

You begin to rely on the feeling of hunger, your body's raucous rebellion at the small tortures of your own hands. When you eventually begin to get well, health will feel wrong, it will make you dizzy, it will confuse you, you will get sick again because sick is what you know.

A Second Look

1. Marya Hornbacher says that eating disorders are "self-perpetuating" (paragraph 3). Why is this so? How does she show us, rather than merely tell us, that her eating disorder "had a life of its own?"

2. How are the eating disorders related to self-esteem and self-image?

3. Besides the unhealthy weight loss, what other physical symptoms does Hornbacher exhibit?

4. The details of Hornbacher's illness make her narrative graphic, powerful, disturbing, and often intense. How does she provide some relief for her readers (and perhaps herself)?

A Cyberlook

1. If you are interested in the subject of eating disorders, you may want to read *Wasted*. To learn more about the book, you can read two reviews on *InfoTrac College Edition*. Go to *Powertrac* and search under the author's

name or the title. You will also find much information on anorexia and bulimia by searching "eating disorders."

2. There are many Internet sites with information about eating disorders. A good place to start (for this or other subjects related to health) is *Internet Mental Health*. Go to that site and click on "Disorders." You will find general descriptions as well as information on diagnosis, treatment, and research. Skim some of the research information to see what is being learned about eating disorders, especially in men (a relatively new field). Compare your results with those of classmates to get an idea of the wide variety of material available. If your instructor wishes, you can work in groups and divide the topics for research. (See *Ideas for Writing*, Number 1.) If you have difficulty finding the site, go to the *Wadsworth Developmental English* web page and click on Textbook Resource Centers.

Ideas for Writing

1. Using the information you collected in your Internet search, write a brief essay on the nature and scope of eating disorders in the United States. Here are some questions to consider: What are the major types of eating disorders? How many people probably suffer from them? What is the relationship between gender and eating disorders? Where is help available? Is there a cure? If your instructor wishes, work in groups with each member taking a subtopic. Then you can write a collaborative report.

2. Have you or has someone you know ever felt, even for a short time, that life was dominated or controlled by a health problem? Describe that experience. Like Marya Hornbacher, you will want to use details that affect your audience, but you will also want to give readers "breathing room."

Talking AIDS to Death

Randy Shilts

Looking Forward

Randy Shilts was for a number of years a leading AIDS activist. A reporter for the *San Francisco Chronicle* and a frequent guest on radio and TV news and talk shows, Shilts became one of the best known spokespersons for advancing AIDS research and treatment. He also wrote several books on AIDS and on gay issues. His best known, the one he was promoting at the time he wrote this essay, is *And the Band Played On: Politics, People, and the AIDS Epidemic* (1987). One of the most interesting aspects of this essay is Shilts's success in blending two narrative lines, one public and one private.

Help with Words

bolstered *(paragraph 1):* strengthened
morass *(paragraph 2):* swamp
retort *(paragraph 5):* sharp reply
insidious *(paragraph 6):* sneaky, treacherous, dangerous but hidden
conspiratorial *(paragraph 7):* characterized by scheming or plotting, secretive
exotic *(paragraph 12):* strange, unusual, foreign
lesions *(paragraph 12):* wounds, a place where tissue is injured
officious *(paragraph 26):* meddlesome, acting official in a pompous and annoying manner
carping *(paragraph 35):* complaining
cornucopia *(paragraph 38):* the horn of plenty; a varied and supply

When Kit Herman was diagnosed with AIDS on May 13, 1989, his doctor leaned over his hospital bed, took his hand, and assured him, "Don't worry, you're in time for AZT." This drug worked so well that all Kit's friends let themselves think he might make it. And we were bolstered by the National Institutes of Health's assurance that AZT was only the first generation of AIDS drugs, and that hundreds of millions of federal dollars going in AIDS treatment research meant there would soon be a second and third generation of treatments to sustain life beyond AZT's effectiveness. Surely nothing was more important, considering the federal government's own estimates that between 1 and 1.5 million Americans were infected with Human Immunodeficiency Virus (HIV), and virtually all would die within the next decade if nothing was done. The new drugs, the NIH assured everyone, were "in the pipeline," and government scientists were working as fast as they possibly could.

Despite my nagging, not one of the dozens of public-affairs show producers chose to look seriously into the development of those long-sought second and third generations of AIDS drugs. In fact, clinical trials of AIDS drugs were hopelessly stalled in the morass of bureaucracy at the NIH, but this story tip never seemed to cut it with producers. Clinical trials were not sexy. Clinical trials were boring.

I made my third *Nightline* appearance in January 1988 because new estimates had been released revealing that one in sixty-one babies born in New York City carried antibodies to the AIDS virus. And the link between those babies and the disease was intravenous drug use by one or both parents. Suddenly, junkies had become the group most likely to catch and spread AIDS through the heterosexual community. Free needles to junkies—now there was a sizzling television topic. I told the show's producers I'd talk about that, but that I was much more interested in the issue of AIDS treatments—which seemed most relevant to the night's program, since Ted Koppel's other guest was Dr. Anthony Fauci, associate NIH director for AIDS, and the administration's most visible AIDS official.

After fifteen minutes of talk on the ins and outs and pros and cons of free needles for intravenous drug users I raised the subject of the pressing need for AIDS treatments. Koppel asked Fauci what was happening. The doctor launched into a discussion of treatments "in the pipeline" and how government scientists were working as fast as they possibly could.

I'd heard the same words from NIH officials for three years: drugs were in the pipeline. Maybe it was true, but when were they going to come out of their goddamn pipeline? Before I could formulate a polite retort to Fauci's stall, however, the segment was over, Ted was thanking us, and the red light on the camera had blipped off. Everyone seemed satisfied that the government was doing everything it possibly could to develop AIDS treatments.

Three months later, I was reading a week-old *New York Times* in Kit's room in the AIDS ward at San Francisco General Hospital. It was April, nearly two years after my friend's AIDS diagnosis. AZT had given him two years of nearly perfect health, but now its effect was wearing off, and Kit had suffered his first major AIDS-related infection since his original bout with pneumonia—cryptococcal meningitis. The meningitis could be treated, we all knew, but the discovery of this insidious brain infection meant more diseases were likely to follow. And the long-promised second and third generations of AIDS drugs were still nowhere on the horizon. While perusing the worn copy of the *Times*, I saw a story about Dr. Fauci's testimony at a congressional hearing. After making Fauci swear an oath to tell the truth, a subcommittee headed by Congressman Ted Weiss of New York City asked why it was taking so long to get new AIDS treatments into testing at a time when Congress was putting hundreds of millions of dollars into NIH budgets for just such purposes. At first Fauci talked about unavoidable delays. He claimed government scientists were working as fast as they could. Pressed harder, he finally admitted that the problem stemmed "almost exclusively" from the lack of staffing in his agency. Congress had allocated funds, it was true, but the Reagan administration had gotten around spending the money by stingily refusing to let Fauci hire anybody. Fauci had requested 127 positions to speed the development of AIDS treatments; the administration had granted him eleven. And for a year, he had not told anyone. For a year, this spokesman for the public health answered reporters that AIDS drugs were in the pipeline and that government scientists had all the money they needed. It seemed that only when faced with the penalty of perjury would one of the administration's top AIDS officials tell the truth. That was the real story, I thought, but for some reason nobody else had picked up on it.

At the international AIDS conference in Stockholm two months later, the other reporters in "the AIDS pack" congratulated me on my success and asked what I was working on now. I admitted that I was too busy promoting the British and German release of my book to do much writing myself, and the next month I had the Australian tour. But if I *were* reporting, I added with a vaguely conspiratorial tone, *I'd* look at the *scandal* in the NIH. Nobody had picked up that New York Times story from a few months ago about staffing shortages on AIDS clinical trials. The lives of 1.5 million HIV-infected Americans hung in the balance, and the only way you could get a straight answer out of an administration AIDS official was to put him under oath and make him face the charges of perjury. Where I went to journalism school, *that* was a news story.

One reporter responded to my tip with the question "But who's going to play you in the miniseries?"

A few minutes later, when Dr. Fauci came into the press room, the world's leading AIDS journalists got back to the serious business of transcribing his remarks. Nobody asked him if he was actually telling the truth, or whether they should put him under oath to ensure a candid response to questions about when we'd get AIDS treatments. Most of the subsequent news accounts of Dr. Fauci's comments faithfully reported that many AIDS treatments were in the pipeline. Government scientists, he said once more, were doing all they possibly could. . . .

"I think I'll make it through this time," Kit said to me, "but I don't have it in me to go through it again."

We were in room 3 of San Francisco General Hospital's ward 5A, the AIDS ward. The poplar trees outside Kit's window were losing their leaves, and the first winter's chill was settling over the city. I was preparing to leave for my fourth and, I hoped, final media tour, this time for release of the book in paperback and on audiocassette; Kit was preparing to die.

The seizures had started a week earlier, indicating he was suffering either from toxoplasmosis, caused by a gluttonous protozoa that sets up housekeeping in the brain; or perhaps it was a relapse of cryptococcal meningitis; or, another specialist guessed, it could be one of those other nasty brain infections that nobody had seen much of until the past year. Now that AIDS patients were living longer, they fell victim to even more exotic infections than in the early days. But the seizures were only part of it. Kit had slowly been losing the sight in his left eye to a herpes infection. And the Kaposi's sarcoma lesions that had scarred his face were beginning to coat the inside of his lungs. When Kit mentioned he'd like to live until Christmas, the doctors said he might want to consider having an early celebration this year, because he wasn't going to be alive in December.

"I can't take another infection," Kit said.

"What does that mean?"

"Morphine," Kit answered, adding mischievously, "lots of it."

We talked briefly about the mechanics of suicide. We both knew people who'd made a mess of it, and people who had done it right. It was hardly the first time the subject had come up in conversation for either of us. Gay men facing AIDS now exchange formulas for suicide as casually as housewives swap recipes for chocolate-chip cookies.

Kit was released from the hospital a few days later. He had decided to take his life on a Tuesday morning. I had to give my first round of interviews in Los Angeles that day, so I stopped on the way to the airport to say goodbye on Monday. All Tuesday, while I gave my perfectly formed sound bites in a round of network radio appearances, I wondered: Is this the moment he's slipping out of consciousness and into that perfect darkness? When I called that night, it turned out he'd delayed his suicide until Thursday to talk to a few more relatives. I had to give a speech in Portland that day, so on the way to the airport I stopped again. He showed me the amber-brown bottle with the bubble-gum-pink morphine syrup, and we said another goodbye.

The next morning, Kit drank his morphine and fell into a deep sleep. That afternoon, he awoke and drowsily asked what time it was. When told it was five hours later, he murmured, "That's amazing. I should have been dead hours ago."

And then he went back to sleep.

That night, Kit woke up again.

"You know what they say about near-death experiences?" he asked. "Going toward the light?"

Shaking his head, he sighed, "No light. Nothing."

His suicide attempt a failure, Kit decided the timing of his death would now be up to God. I kept up on the bizarre sequence of events by phone and called as soon as I got back to San Francisco. I was going to tell Kit that his theme song should be "Never Can Say Goodbye," but then the person on the other end of the phone told me that Kit had lapsed into a coma.

The next morning, he died.

Kit's death was like everything about AIDS—anticlimactic. By the time he actually did die, I was almost beyond feeling.

The next day I flew to Boston for the start of the paperback tour, my heart torn between rage and sorrow. All week, as I was chauffeured to my appearances on *Good Morning America, Larry King Live,* and various CNN shows, I kept thinking, It's all going to break. I'm going to be on a TV show with some officious government health spokesman lying to protect his job, and I'm going to start shouting, "You lying son of a bitch. Don't you know there are people, real people, people I love out there dying?" Or I'll be on a call-in show and another mother will phone about her thirty-seven-year-old son who just died and it will hit me all at once, and I'll start weeping.

But day after day as the tour went on, no matter how many official lies I heard and how many grieving mothers I talked to, the crack-up never occurred. All my answers came out rationally in tight little sound bites about institutional barriers to AIDS treatments and projections about 1993 case loads.

By the last day of the tour, when a limousine picked me up at my Beverly Hills hotel for my last round of satellite TV interviews, I knew I had to stop. In a few weeks I'd return to being national correspondent for the *Chronicle,* and it was time to get off the AIDS celebrity circuit, end the interviews and decline the invitations to the star-studded fund raisers, and get back to work as a newspaper reporter. That afternoon, there was just one last radio interview to a call-in show in the San Fernando Valley, and then it would be over.

The first caller asked why his tax money should go toward

funding an AIDS cure when people got the disease through their own misdeeds.

I used my standard jukebox answer about how most cancer cases are linked to people's behavior but that nobody ever suggested we stop trying to find a cure for cancer.

A second caller phoned to ask why her tax money should go to finding an AIDS cure when these people clearly deserved what they got.

I calmly put a new spin on the same answer, saying in America you usually don't sentence people to die for having a different lifestyle from yours.

Then a third caller phoned in to say that he didn't care if all those queers and junkies died, as did a fourth and fifth and sixth caller. By then I was shouting, "You stupid bigot. You just want to kill off everybody you don't like. You goddamn Nazi."

The talk-show host sat in stunned silence. She'd heard I was so *reasonable*. My anger baited the audience further, and the seventh and eighth callers began talking about "you guys" as if only a faggot like myself could give a shit about whether AIDS patients all dropped dead tomorrow. . . .

When I got home to San Francisco that night, I looked over some notes I had taken from a conversation I'd had with Kit during his last stay in the hospital. I was carping about how frustrated I was at the prospect of returning to my reporting job. If an internationally acclaimed best seller hadn't done shit to change the world, what good would mere newspaper stories do?

"The limits of information," Kit said. "There's been a lot written on it."

"Oh," I said.

Kit closed his eyes briefly and faded into sleep while plastic tubes fed him a cornucopia of antibiotics. After five minutes, he stirred, looked up, and added, as if we had never stopped talking, "But you don't really have a choice. You've got to keep on doing it. What else are you going to do?"

AFTERWORD

In 1994, after years of writing and speaking about the AIDS crisis and other gay issues, Randy Shilts died of AIDS. He was 42. Among many memorial statements about Shilts, one of the most widely known is

Block 3780 of the AIDS Quilt. This block is on permanent display on the Aids Quilt web site.

A Second Look

1. Randy Shilts records two related narratives—the illness and death of his friend Kit and his growing frustration and anger at the lack of progress in AIDS research and treatment. How does he weave these narratives together?

2. In paragraphs 1, 4, 5, 6, and 9, Shilts repeats (with minor changes) two phrases: new drugs were "in the pipeline" and government scientists were "working as fast as they possibly could." Why do you think he uses such repetition? What is its effect?

3. When Shilts continues the promotional tour for his book after his friend's death, he fears that "It's all going to break" (paragraph 26). It finally does. What pushes him over the edge into an angry counterattack on callers to the radio talk show?

4. At the end of his essay, Shilts writes again of his friend Kit, recalling a conversation they had shortly before Kit died. Shilts feels that his continued reporting on the AIDS crisis is useless, that he is not accomplishing anything. His friend says Shilts has no choice but to keep on: "What else are you going to do?" Do you think this open question is an effective conclusion to the essay? Why or why not?

A Cyberlook

1. AIDS research continues, but so does the debate over the federal government's pace and degree of support. For recent information on this topic, go to *InfoTrac College Edition* and search "AIDS Research." You can also search "AIDS" and find many subdivisions, including AIDS in children.

2. The number of Internet sites on AIDS is enormous, and the type and quality of information varies greatly. For information links and a good reading list, go to the HIV/AIDS site maintained by the University of Wisconsin-Oshkosh. You can also get an idea of the scope and direction of research by going to the site *HIV/AIDS Evaluation and Research WWW Links*. Examine some of these links and compare your results with those of classmates. If you have difficulty finding the site, go to the *Wadsworth Developmental English* web page and click on Textbook Resource Centers.

Ideas for Writing

1. Many people find that in the face of tragedy or life-threatening circumstances of friends and loved ones, they must continue what looks like everyday life. This is a painful but common experience. If you or someone you know has faced this situation, describe it in an essay. Show readers how the person being described coped with the ordinary routine of his or her life while dealing with extraordinary circumstances. It may be that, as in Randy Shilts's case, the two paths of experience intersect.

2. Using information from your Internet search, prepare a report on the current status of AIDS research. If your instructor wishes, you can work on this in groups. The report could also be prepared for oral presentation.

Driving Drunk

Cecilia Kirtley

Looking Forward

Everyone knows the dangers of mixing alcohol and automobiles, but this knowledge becomes personal and painful for those whose lives are changed by alcohol-related accidents. In this essay, Cecilia Kirtley tells how, as a college student who is already familiar with the usual facts and statistics, she is suddenly faced with the reality of death at the hands of a drunk driver—not once, but twice. The names of the persons involved have been changed.

Help with Words

inevitable *(paragraph 6):* certain, unavoidable

Ring, ring. "Hello," I answered, half asleep. "She's dead, she's dead," I thought I heard a voice scream. My first thought was that someone was calling to tell me that my sister had been killed, but I was wrong. I had misunderstood the person on the phone. The hysterical person whose voice I heard *was* my sister. She was saying, "He's dead, he's dead." The boy she was dating had been killed by a drunk driver who was going the wrong way on the expressway. Imagine this happening to someone in your family. Imagine, as a college student, getting a call late one night telling you that your friend, roommate, sister, brother, or even your parents had been killed in a drunk driving accident. Driving drunk endangers not only the drunk drivers themselves but all the innocent people around them. These people could be the loved ones in your life.

As I look back on that night, I remember that feeling of my heart dropping to my feet while my emotions raced from fear to uncontrollable distress. The scary fact is that many people have to deal with this horrible reality in their lives. More than 16,000 people a year are killed in the United States in car crashes involving alcohol. That comes to four times as many Americans dying in drunk driving crashes as were killed in the Vietnam War. These facts reflect the true reality of drinking and driving, not some story book version. Consider how many people have had to receive that call saying that someone they cared about was dead.

Now reflect on another situation. A young, beautiful college freshman named Sara went to a party. She had decided not to drink. She had been taught that when you are going to drive a car, you do not use alcohol. She had a great time sober, and as the party began to wind down, she went to her car and hopped in. She was glad that she had listened to her conscience and decided to be smart. She knew that she would make it back to her dorm room safe. As she pulled out, she began to sing along with a favorite song that had just come on the radio. Out of nowhere she saw lights coming straight at her. Within seconds she was lying on the pavement in a pool of blood—her own blood.

Sara's roommate Emily, one of my good friends, is getting a call that will change her life forever. Emily gets the same call I received, but this time she understands the caller correctly. Her best friend and roommate has lost her life because of another college student's failure to think and act responsibly.

Statistically, 240,000 to 360,000 of the nation's 12 million undergraduate students could die from alcohol-related causes. Students need to consider that when they drink and drive, they endanger not only their lives, but the lives of their friends. Many students do not take this seriously. More than one-third—35.6%—of college students have admitted driving while under the influence. Since both of the accidents I have described occurred in the morning hours, there is another statistic we must consider. Between 1:00 a.m. and 6:00 a.m. on weekend mornings, one in seven drivers is drunk. That's a scary statistic! Do you really want to be the one in seven who drives drunk and possibly takes the life of another?

As college students, we must work to assure that this does not happen on our campuses. It is inevitable that college students will drink. Forty-two percent of all college students report that they engage in binge drinking (five or more drinks at a time) in a two-week period. Even though it may be impossible to change this statistic dramatically, we can try to prevent tragedies due to drinking and driving. We can admit to ourselves that once friends start drinking, they probably won't stop at a safe limit. We can take those friends' keys away after the first drink. We can get students to voice their disapproval of drinking and driving. SADD (Students Against Drinking and Driving) should be a part of all college campuses.

We must try to stop valuable lives from being lost because people choose to drive while intoxicated. Education is the best way to make people see the true danger of their actions. No one has the right to take a life just because he or she chooses to take the keys, get in a car, and drive drunk.

A Second Look

1. Evaluate Cecilia Kirtley's introduction. Is the opening illustration effective? Why or why not?

2. How does Kirtley actively involve her readers in her experience and in her discussion of preventive measures?

3. Why does the writer shift from past tense in paragraph 3 to present tense in paragraph 4? Is this an effective technique?

4. When Kirtley sums up her persuasive thesis in paragraphs 6 and 7, her argument is that college students *will* continue to drink, so the best course of action is to educate those who drink and drive and, when necessary, to intervene. Basically, she says we cannot eliminate the cause; we can only work to alter the effects. Is this a good argumentative strategy? Why or why not?

A Cyberlook

1. One evening Lisa Wright, a seventeen-year-old high school cheerleader, went riding with her boyfriend and some other friends. All were

drinking. A few hours later, Lisa was a crash victim in the trauma unit of a nearby hospital. A year and a half later Lisa, by then a paraplegic college student confined to a wheelchair, was able to write about her experience in order to share it with others. To read her account of the accident and how she reacted to it, access *InfoTrac College Edition,* go to *Powertrac,* click on the title index, and enter "Lisa's Story."

2. If you search "drunk driving" on the Internet, you will find everything from organizations against drunk driving to state laws regulating alcohol consumption to attorneys who solicit DUI clients online. Much information, mostly of a practical kind, can be found on the site maintained by MADD (Mothers Against Drunk Driving). Another excellent site, especially for college students, is that maintained by SADD (now Students Against Destructive Decisions). Working alone or in small groups, search "drinking on campus." Compare your results.

Ideas for Writing

We often read narratives of people who are seriously injured in accidents but who make great efforts to recover to the degree possible and to move their altered lives forward. If you know someone who has done this, tell his or her story. What happened to this person? What was the recovery like? How has the person adapted and moved into his or her new life? You will need to use limited but effective details, so write down as much information as you can in the planning stage and then choose carefully the material you think will most interest and affect your readers.

Why Would Anyone Want to Smoke?

Courtney Fugate

Looking Forward

Courtney Fugate has seen firsthand the terrible effects that prolonged smoking can cause. In this student essay, she uses statistics, concrete medical details, facts about everyday hygiene, and especially her personal experiences to build a strong case against tobacco use.

Help with Words

impressionable *(paragraph 1):* easily affected, sensitive
carcinogenic *(paragraph 3):* cancer-causing

My mom slowly pushed open the heavy metal door of the hospital's intensive care unit. All was quiet except for the humming and beeping of the various monitors and machines hooked up to the patients. I followed her to the left corner of the room where my dad lay, recovering from double by-pass surgery and partial foot amputation. He had over two hundred metal staples up and down his arm and legs. His left foot was wrapped in a thick, white gauze bandage where his first two toes and a portion of the foot had been removed. My dad had tubes and needles running into his body in every possible place to help him breathe and to administer pain medication. If he had only had the strength to quit smoking, he could have spared himself and my family the pain we all would endure. This was the second in a series of operations that would eventually lead to the amputation of his leg just below the knee. Witnessing firsthand everything my dad had to go through impacted me in a way I will never forget. It was an experience that, at the impressionable age of twelve, made me promise to myself that I would never have anything to do with cigarette smoking.

Why would anyone want to smoke cigarettes? The health risks caused by smoking seem endless, not to mention the many other ways tobacco can negatively affect one's life. Cigarette smoking is the most preventable cause of premature death in the United States today, yet smoking kills more than 400,000 Americans a year. Since 1964, when the Surgeon General's report on smoking was first published, nearly ten million people have died from causes related to tobacco. The personal health risks associated with smoking are immeasurable. It can cause heart disease, emphysema, various types of cancer, chronic obstructive pulmonary disease, and atherosclerosis, among other things. The risk of lung cancer in men who smoke increases twenty-two times. On average, smokers die seven years earlier than non-smokers. We can add that the personal hygiene of a smoker is also adversely affected. The smoker's teeth and nails turn yellow, he develops smoker's breath, and his clothes smell of tobacco smoke.

And it is not only the smoker's personal health and hygiene that are affected by tobacco smoking. Passive or second-hand smoke is responsible for 53,000 deaths annually in the United States. Cigarette smoke contains over 4,000 chemicals, many that are carcinogenic. People around smokers, even if they do not smoke themselves, are exposed to many of the same health risks as the smoker. Infants and children are perhaps those most often affected. If a pregnant mother smokes, her child has an increased chance of being born with respiratory problems, heart disease, and low birth weight. Smoking during pregnancy also increases the chance of miscarriage, premature birth, and stillbirth. Children of smokers have more chronic respiratory problems and are sick more often than children of non-smokers. Think about these things the next time you light up next to a non-smoker or the next time you allow a smoker to light up around you.

Health risks are not the only negative consequences of cigarette smoking. The feelings and well-being of a smoker's family and friends must be considered. Watching my father change over the years from an active, happy man to someone who rarely goes out much and is clinically depressed has not been easy. The financial stability of my family has been greatly affected because my dad, who is self-employed, cannot work as much or as often as he could before the amputation. Watching my grandmother die of lung cancer was not easy either.

Still, it is painful and hard to get the message to my parents. Even after all they have been through, they continue to smoke. I want them to be around when my children are born and grow up. I want them to be a part of my life for a long time. However, if they cannot beat their addiction to nicotine, the chances of that are very slim. Consider these things if you smoke or if you are thinking about starting. You will be harming many people in addition to yourself.

A Second Look

1. Courtney Fugate's opening paragraph is quiet. There is limited activity; there is little sound, and no one speaks. Why is this style appropriate to the subject matter? Do you think this is a successful way to open the essay? Why or why not?

2. In paragraphs 3 and 5, Fugate addresses her readers directly as "you." This is a stylistic technique that student writers are usually advised *not* to use. Would you advise the writer to revise these paragraphs, eliminating the second person pronouns? Explain your answer.

3. In persuasive writing, emotional appeal is an honest and effective tool if it is used responsibly and combined with factual material. How does Fugate combine emotional and factual arguments? Which personal and non-personal information do you consider most effective?

A Cyberlook

1. King James I hated tobacco but found the crop too profitable to ban. In Colonial America, some Puritan leaders outlawed the use of tobacco,

probably because they realized that smoking gave pleasure. Tobacco was once thought to cure cancer. Mark Twain made it a rule "never to smoke when asleep, and never to refrain when awake." To learn more about these and other fascinating tidbits from the history of tobacco, see Stephen Good, "Call it a 'stinking weed,' just don't try to ban it" on *InfoTrac College Edition*. Search *Powertrac* by author or title.

2. For recent general information on the tobacco controversy (as well as other health-related topics), see *Prevention Primer*, one of the sites of the National Clearinghouse for Alcohol and Drug Information. Go to the site, click on "T," then on "Tobacco." Another good resource is the site called *Argumentative Essay Topics*. See *Ideas for Writing*, Number 1. If you have difficulty finding the site, go to the *Wadsworth Developmental English* web page and click on Textbook Resource Centers.

Ideas for Writing

1. One of the hottest topics in the debate over the use of tobacco is advertising, especially that which targets children and teens. Write your own argumentative/persuasive essay on this subject using your own knowledge and experience supported by material gathered on the Internet. An excellent place to begin is *Argumentative Essay Topics*, a site maintained by the Maricopa Community Colleges (AZ). Here you can also access online help in writing your paper by clicking on the link *Argumentative Essay Web Site*.

2. Cecilia Kirtley and Courtney Fugate both write about health-related topics, using statistics, factual information, and personal experience. Write a paper in which you compare and contrast their essays. What are the similarities in the way their essays are put together? What is similar and different about their introductions and conclusions? How do the writers use their personal experiences? Which do you, as a reader, find more effective?

Making Connections

Cecilia Kirtley and Courtney Fugate are college students writing about recent experiences. Marya Hornbacher was a student during much of the time she describes in *Wasted*. Do these writers describe unusual, atypical experiences, or do college students directly or indirectly face a disturbing assortment of health-related issues? Should colleges and universities take more time to educate students about their health, or is this primarily a personal responsibility? If you realized that a friend had a health problem that he or she was unwilling or unable to deal with alone, would you intervene?

Acknowledgments

Maxine Hong Kingston. "The Woman Warrior," from *The Woman Warrior: Memoirs of a Girlhood Among Ghosts* by Maxine Hong Kingston. Copyright © 1975, 1976 by Maxine Hong Kingston. Reprinted by permission of Alfred A. Knopf, Inc.

Piri Thomas. "Down These Mean Streets," from *Down These Mean Streets* by Piri Thomas. Copyright © 1967 by Piri Thomas. Reprinted by permission of Alfred A. Knopf, Inc.

John C. Bennett. "My First Hunting Trip." Reprinted by permission of John C. Bennett.

Richard Rodriguez. "My Family's Language," from *Hunger of Memory* by Richard Rodriguez. Reprinted by permission of David R. Godine, Publisher, Inc. Copyright © 1982 by Richard Rodriguez.

Colette Dowling. "Becoming Helpless" from *The Cinderella Complex*, copyright © 1981 by Colette Dowling.

Garrison Keillor. "After a Fall." Copyright © 1982 by Garrison Keillor, originally appeared in *The New Yorker*, from *Happy to Be Here* by Garrison Keillor.

"Halfway to Dick and Jane" by Jack Agueros, copyright © 1971 by Doubleday, a division of Bantam Doubleday Dell Publishing Group, Inc., from THE IMMIGRANT EXPERIENCE by Thomas C. Wheeler. Used by permission of Doubleday, a division of Random House, Inc.

David Raymond. "On Being Seventeen, Bright, and Unable to Read." Copyright © 1976 by The New York Times. Reprinted by permission.

Lewis P. Johnson. "For My Indian Daughter," from *Newsweek*, September 5, 1983. Copyright © 1983 by *Newsweek*. All rights reserved.

Stephen King. "Head Down." *The New Yorker*, April 16, 1990. © 1990 Stephen King. Reprinted by permission of *The New Yorker*.

Arthur Ashe. "Send Your Children to the Libraries." Copyright © 1977 by The New York Times. Reprinted by permission.

John Updike. "Ex-Basketball Player," from *The Carpentered Hen and Other Tame Creatures* by John Updike. Copyright © 1957, 1982 by John Updike. Reprinted by permission of Alfred A. Knopf, Inc.

"Comes the Revolution," *Time* Magazine, June 26, 1978. © 1978 by Time, Inc. All rights reserved. Reprinted by permission of Time.

Ellen Goodman. "The Company Man," from *At Large* by Ellen Goodman. Copyright © 1981 by Washington Post Co.

Roger Rosenblatt. "Out of Work in America," *Life* Magazine, August 1991. © 1991 The Time Inc. Magazine Company.

Pete Axthelm. "Where Have All the Heroes Gone?" Copyright 1979 by Newsweek, Inc. Reprinted by permission.

Maya Angelou. **"I Know Why the Caged Bird Sings,"** from *I Know Why the Caged Bird Sings* by Maya Angelou. Copyright © 1969 by Maya Angelou. Reprinted by permission of Alfred A. Knopf, Inc.

Rich Weiss. **"Significant Other,"** *The New York Times,* September 1, 1991. Copyright © 1991 by The New York Times. Reprinted by permission.

Randy Shilts. **"Talking AIDS to Death,"** *Esquire* Magazine, March 1989, p. 126–128, and p. 132–135. © 1989 by Randy Shilts.

Photo Credits

p. 86, © Jim Fossett/The Image Works; p. 158, Mike Okoniewski/The Image Works